THREE SHORT PLAYS

Translated and adapted from the works of Anton Chekhov,

by

Elizabeth Gamberoni.

"THE SUMMER OF THE ECLIPSE"

Translated and adapted from a short story:
"Notes from the Journal of a Quick-tempered Man."

"THE DENTAL SURGEON"

Translated and adapted from an early burlesque:
"The Surgeon."

"SWANSONG"

Translated and adapted from a *"Curtain Raiser,"*

(which has been previously translated and performed in
Britain.)

JUVENTUS Publications include:
From *The Italian Girl* to *Cabaret* (1998)
Romanticism & Melody (1995)

First published in 1998 by JUVENTUS, 81 Lumley Courtyard,
Holbein Place, London SW1W 8LU

Application for professional or amateur performace of these plays
should be made before rehearsal to:

The Butterfly Prawn Company,
16, Kensington Hall Gardens,
Beaumont Avenue,
London W14 9LS

British Library Cataloguing-in-Publication Data

A catalogue record for this book
is available from the British Library

ISBN 0 9524964 45

Cover by Mark Hedge
Typeset by York House Typographic
Printed and bound by J. W. Arrowsmith Ltd, Bristol

NOTES ON THE LIFE OF CHEKHOV

by

Elizabeth Gamberoni

Anton-Pavlovich Chekhov was born on January 17th, 1860 in Taganrog, a small port in Southern Russia. He belonged neither to the aristocracy, nor the middle-class, nor to the intelligentsia which he so vividly portrayed. His maternal grandfather was a former serf who had bought himself out twenty years before the Emancipation in 1861. Chekhov's father, Pavel (Paul) owned a small shop which sold everything from tea, coffee, candles, penknives, hair oil, and alcohol – to quack medicines.

It might be as well to explain patronymics here to English readers who become so irritated by the lengthy names in Russian literature. *Ovich*, or *ich* at the end of a christian name simply means 'son of', e.g. Anton-Pavlovich Chekhov, means Anthony, son of Paul: *evna* means 'daughter of', e.g. Maria-Pavlevna Chekhov, (Chekhov's beloved sister) means Mary, daughter of Paul. It is amazing how few people seem to be aware of this fact, including, (to my ASTONISHMENT,) many seasoned actors who have appeared in Chekhov and Turgenev's plays.

Pavel Chekhov had six children, the third being Anton. Pavel was a tall good-looking man, and a strict disciplinarian, feared by his wife and children. Speaking at mealtimes, or any other slight misdemeanor, meant a severe flogging. When his wife tried to intervene, his answer was: 'That was the way I was brought up and it did me no harm.' If the meal was late, or the soup over-salted, a tyrannical rage would follow, which terrified each member of the family. There were, however, positive sides to his nature; he read music, was a good violonist, and quite gifted at painting ikons. His second son Nikolai beame a talented painter, his son Alexander was initially a very talented writer, (but largely thanks to womanizing and drink ended up as a hack-writer,) and his daughter Maria became a dedicated teacher. Chekhov later said of him: 'We inherited our talents from our father, and our soul from our mother'.

Pavel's unheated shop was open from five in the morning till midnight and from an early age Anton was forced to work there. Shuddering with cold he tried to keep abreast of his homework, for he was behind at school, but as the ink in the inkwell had frequently frozen solid, this was not possible. Free time as such did not exist, for Pavel had become a choirmaster enrolling all his sons in the choir where they practised as much as three hours a day. A wrong note, or stifled yawn was rewarded by a thump around the ear. Services in the Russian Orthodox Church are extremely lengthy – they can go on for several hours and often take place early in the morning or sometimes very late at night. Pavel – a religious fanatic attended all of these with his children, and perhaps as a result of his father's 'devotions', Chekhov was to become an agnostic, although he retained a deep love of church rituals and music. Writing to a friend many years later he said: 'Childhood? I had none!'

Amazingly, Anton remained fond of his bigoted father to the end of his life, by which time the old man had somewhat softened.

With this harsh upbringing it is small wonder that throughout Chekhov's life, he was plagued by ill-health, culminating in his death from tubercolosis at the age of 44.

Taganrog, with its port, was a fairly prosperous small town, with many of its businesses owned by Greeks, Italians, Turks, the French and British who lived in far greater luxury than the indigenous Russians who mainly existed in shacks, did manual work in the docks, or ran small shops like Pavel. Taganrog was proud of its small theatre, built by the Italians in which well known artistes appeared: this gave Chekhov his first glimpse and lasting love of the theatre. He always enjoyed playing charades, and was a brilliant mimic.

The town which Chekhov wrote about many times, had the Crimea on its western shore, and the Seas of Azov, linked by a channel to the Black Sea which gave it a valuable trading route to Turkey and the Mediterranean. However, this was the age of the railway, and an important terminal had been built at Rostov-on-

Don, a much larger trading city nearby on the estuary of the Don, to which Taganrog was to lose much of its business. The reason was that the leading tradesmen had turned down the proposal to fund a branch line to Taganrog because of the heavy cost/bribe involved, and settled for a branch line fourteen miles OUTSIDE the town, figuring (wrongly) that the cost of building a road to the station would be cheaper. As a result many foreign vessels refused to call there, the harbour became silted up, and commerce foreseeably declined, affecting the livelihood of its citizens, and especially its poorer inhabitants.

Pavel moved his shop closer to the station, where he hoped to get custom from passing travellers. This was not so, he lost out to larger concerns. At the same time the family moved from rented accomodation to a bigger house he had had built to accomodate his growing family, and hopefully take in lodgers. Never an astute businessman, he was defrauded by the builders. He was also not very bright about the children's education. Ignoring, as he always did, his wife's more practical advice he chose a Greek school for Anton and Nikolai, hoping that mixing with them – even the poorer Greeks, would help them learn their business acumen, (the Greeks being among the richest inhabitants of Taganrog) thus increasing their opportunities in later life. This was not to be the case! The lessons were all in Greek, and the Greek students ragged them unmercifully about their pronunciation and as a result they lost over a year's schooling because of Pavel's opposition to the gymnasium, (the school his wife favoured) where they would receive a classical Russian education along with children from the middle class. They were finally sent to the gymnasium, and ultimately to university.

As business in the shop declined, Chekhov noticed his father becoming increasingly morose and violent. Pavel had borrowed a large sum to build the house, which had not been repaid by 1876, and he was threatened with the Debtor's Prison. In comically humiliating circumstances, he had to flee from Taganrog, hidden in a cart, and took a train many miles from the local station to a secret address in Moscow – where, optimistically, he hoped to launch a further business enterprise. There was more than a touch of Mr Micawber in Pavel Chekhov's character.

Some weeks later, Chekhov's mother left for Moscow with her other children (Alexander, the eldest, was already at university there) taking only the possessions they could carry, and leaving behind Anton as a sort of hostage to work for one of Pavel's creditors who had bought the house and shop. He aso had to tutor the owner's children at a cheap rate, as well as doing a bit of tailoring. (Another of Pavel's earlier brilliant ideas was that Anton should master this craft.)

They were an extremely close-knit family, and Anton was desperately lonely and worried, missing his brothers, sister, mother, and even father. He remained alone for three years till he graduated, continuing his odd jobs, and even took on tutoring a further three students so that he could send on piecemeal the family's few remaining possessions, including his mother's sewing machine. He also, through a rich Moscow cousin secretly sent his mother money, as the family's only income was the few roubles she earned from sewing. Pavel had found a very poorly paid job outside Moscow, and was only able to visit his family twice a month.

At nineteen Anton graduated with sufficient marks to gain a small grant towards his fees to the Medical Faculty in Moscow. As soon as he arrived he took over the family's affairs, having a great deal of common sense, and because his older brothers Alexander and Nikolai were into *la vie bohème*, drinking heavily, and providing little in the way of financial help. The family soon moved to a larger flat and this was achieved by inviting two rich student friends who had graduated with Anton to board there. It was then that Chekhov began writing to earn money. Alexander was already gaining a name with his writing, and with his help, Anton began selling jokes and stories to comic magazines, the work of both brothers being illustrated by Nikolai, a talented artist, who died at 31 of tuberculosis.

Anton continued turning out these jokes (under the name of Chekhonte) until after he got his medical degree. He began to gain a reputation, attracted the attention of a newspaper proprietor, Aleksei Suvorin, and started writing short stories, and a newspaper column for his newspaper, *New Time*. Although Suvorin was far older, they formed a deep friendship, corresponded regularly, and frequently travelled abroad together. Many were surprised by this friendhsip, since Suvorin and especially his two sons had extremely reactionary views, whereas Chekhov believed in artistic and political freedom and was against any extreme movement, be it left or right.

For many years, Chekhov did not take himself seriously as a writer – he did it merely to pay the bills. But Suvorin, a generous man, appreciated his talent and gave him great encouragement, as well as helping provide him with a degree of economic stability. However, Chekhov, being of a benevolent nature – almost a soft touch, always lived well beyond his means. Once he was established, he funded schools, libraries and hospitals, where he acted as an unpaid medical adviser. He was a true humanitarian, even paying for the education of the daughter of a man who had worked in his father's small shop in Taganrog.

Unlike most authors, Chekhov was encouraging to young writers, praising what he liked, and criticizing – not destructively – what he felt didn't work. He became very close to Maxim Gorki, and helped him rework many of this plays. Ivan Bunin, almost my favourite Russian writer next to Chekhov, was another dear friend.

In 1892 he moved the family to Melikhova, 50 miles south of Moscow. He remained there for six years, with frequent visits to his beloved Moscow, and it was probably the most creative period of his life.

As the tubercolosis accelerated, his heart became weak and because of increasing bouts of asthma his doctors ordered him to stay away from Moscow – especially in winter, and move to the warm south. He had a house built in Yalta, with a huge garden, for he loved gardening, and travelled a great deal for treatment to Austria, Germany and France often with Suvorin, and their close friendship continued until the Dreyfus Affair. After a severe attack, and many weeks spent in hospital in Moscow, Chekhov went to Nice to recuperate, and he was there in 1898 when Zola's trial began. The *New Time* in Russia published a series of virulent, blatantly anti-semitic attacks on Zola, and Chekhov wrote from Nice, expressing his dismay at the way the paper had dealt with the case. Suvorin frequently wrote to him expressing a sort of repentance, and for some years they went on meeting and corresponding, although Chekhov soon ceased to write for the paper. However, the Dreyfus Affair which had divided people all over the world, effectively marked the end of their once very warm and valued friendship.

Tolstoi, who also had a house in Yalta, was a friend of Chekhov's and a great admirer of his short stories – comparing him with Maupassant. Tolstoi was an aristocrat, immensely successful, and probably the best known man in Russia. Chekhov had immense respect for him, not just as a writer but because of his sympathetic attitude towards the poor. However after a few years he found some of his ideas, especially his view of the 'noble peasants', to be somewhat simplistic and it began to irritate him. Chekhov had lived and worked with peasants all his life and he knew they could be violent, uncouth, stingy and uncaring, as well as 'good and noble.' He drew characters in the round – rich and poor, which is what makes him such a superb observer of human nature.

Tolstoi was NOT impressed with Chekhov's plays, and said: 'He writes even worse plays than Shakespeare' (for whom he had little respect). Anton was delighted when he heard this, and laughed so much that his pince-nez fell off.

Chekhov was a man of fashion, and – an endearing weakness – loved having his photograph taken. Nowadays one thinks of pince-nez as being worn only by old fogeys. This was not the case; they were the height of fashion, rather as John Lennon's granny specs were to become in our lifetime.

It is a sad thing that in this country he is principally known for his plays, some of which are in danger of being done to death, and not always in the best of productions – expensive maybe, but they neither look nor feel Chekhovian. In fact he was a prolific prose writer of over 600 stories, and some are ranked among the world's very greatest. Sadly, many of the tales written in his early years have disappeared.

Many considered him to be a pessimist, a criticism which

wounded him deeply. He saw life as it was, warts and all, but considered himself an optimist; he enjoyed company, adored entertaining, and clearly had great faith in the future. Performed as intended, his plays should teeter on a knife's edge between comedy and tragedy. He didn't see eye to eye with Stanislavski on many things, hardly surprising this, since Stanislavski was a didactic, self-satisfied humourless man. Chekhov admired him as an actor, but didn't often agree with Stanislavski's conception of his plays finding them over-histrionic, and lacking in humour.

However, I can well understand why Stanislavski thought of *Uncle Vanya* as a tragedy. True to life – yes! But I personally feel that a government health warning should be issued with every production: "Do NOT see this play if your are over 25, unless you have had a singularly happy and fulfilled life."

I have adapted *The Summer of the Eclipse* from a comic short story *Notes from the Journal of a Quick-tempered Man*, and his writings on the Russian landscape. It highlights his sense of the ridiculous – the pedantic middle-aged hero, Nikolai, trying to make a name for himself in the annals of science by recording his impressions of the eclipse of the sun, and his efforts to involve his less 'committed' neighbours. The play also stresses Chekhov's deep love of nature and obsession with conservation – a theme he returned to many times – Doctor Astrov in *Uncle Vanya* expressed some of his fears. From 1900 onward, many other Russian writers were obsessed by this fear, and when one sees the continuing destruction of the rain forests, the pollution of the oceans and that ever-growing hole in the ozone layer, one realises how foresighted they were.

Many of the characters Chekhov used in his plays come from his short stories. The primitive surgery in the back of beyond in *The Dental Surgeon* was no exaggeration, but based on the people and situations he encountered when practising medicine – for which he was rarely paid. This short piece was written as a burlesque, He was writing these curtain raisers for actors and music halls many years before he began seriously writing for the theatre, and when reading them one can tell he had not yet mastered the technique, since many of the best lines are in the stage directions, e.g. Kooryatin (the Ward Orderly) enters smoking a foul-smelling cigar. Question. How does one convey that to an audience? Answer, you have to invent dialogue. The original title was The Surgeon, but I renamed it, since some people are unaware that purely Dental Surgeons as such, in 1884, were very thin upon the ground. Troublesome molars were either yanked out by a doctor, more often a barber, or indeed anyone with strong wrists. Failing that, there was always of course (especially for the poor) the time-honoured method of tying a piece of string around the offending tooth, attaching it to a doorknob, and then slamming the door.

He wrote another hilarious story about raging toothache called *A horsey-sounding Name*, which has gone into the Russian language as an idiom for when you can't recall a name. Where, in English, we would say, 'You know – whats-his name, or, thingummyjig', they say 'You know – a horsey-sounding name' without realizing perhaps they are quoting directly from Chekhov. I won't tell you the plot of that story for fear of spoiling the joke.

Swansong has been previously translated into English. Mostly it is treated as a straight-forward comedy, and indeed it is funny. Svetlovidov, an immensely vain, once-great actor is on yet another 'final farewell tour,' appearing at a fourth-rate theatre in the provinces, where he wakes up alone at three in the morning after a drunken binge, and looks back on his life. There are only two roles in this play, Svetlovidov, and Nikita, the promptmaster. What I dislike most in the productions I have seen, is that Nikita is played as a yokel, a sort of clichéd two-dimensional Oirish Idyat. Bearing in mind that only about 40 per cent of Russians were literate at that time, he would be quite well-educated, and knows the classics by heart. I see him as a failed actor, who sees in Svetlovidov the artist he could never have become. Therefore his admiration is truly genuine, 'Genius! Such talent!!' I also feel Nikita would be slightly camp. Take Svetlovidov's lines:

'Home? I've no home to go to … I've no wife, nor children …'

Nikita interrupts, 'Oo now – there's a thing to grieve about.'

Of course Svetlovidov DOES go over the top, especially when describing his life and becoming mesmerized by his own eloquence. He can barnstorm with the best. However there IS something tragic to me about a once-great actor, who knows he's wasted his talent, and is now at the end of the road.

Writing to a woman friend in 1887 Chekhov mentions *Swansong* at the end of his letter:

'I have written a play on four sheets of paper ... On the whole little things are much better to write than big ones, there is very little pretension and sure success. I wrote my drama in one hour and five minutes. I started another, but didn't finish it, for I had no time ...'

A mere hour and five minutes – in LONGHAND at that! Dear God!! What hope for other writers? In *Swansong*, the old actor Svetlovidov quotes many speeches from Shakespeare, whose work Chekhov greatly admired. On the advice of a very experienced classical actor, I have lengthened some of the Shakespearian speeches to their logical conclusion, and if Chekhov had had more than 65 minutes at his disposal, I feel certain he would have done the same thing, for he revised many of his earlier works. Indeed he allotted the task of tracking down his early stories to a woman who loved him deeply, so that he could bring them up to scratch or destroy them as he saw fit, and also, probably, get her out of his hair. Anton was not a womanizer, but many women found him attractive.

He married Olga Knipper, an actress from the Moscow Art Theatre in 1901 after she had proposed to him. They had been having an affair for some time, during which she often visited his home in Yalta and seems to have had a good relationship with his sister. The marriage was happy, although they spent little time together – she would be acting in Moscow, whilst he worked/recuperated in Yalta or abroad. Olga was a committed and talented actress who enjoyed partying, and Chekhov's health at that time prevented him from spending much time in Moscow and staying up late. Would the marriage have lasted in different circumstances? I don't know. I well remember some elderly Russians telling me rather tartly many years ago: 'She was a very selfish woman – wasn't prepared to sacrifice herself, and Chekhov was after all a great catch. Next to Tolstoi, he was the most famous and revered man in all Russia.'

However, judging from his letters to Olga, (for they frequently corresponded,) it seems to have been a happy marriage. He liked independent women, and had in the past clearly discouraged permanent ties. They wanted children, and Olga miscarried twice. Some – spitefully perhaps – attributed it to her hectic life-style.

Olga was with him when he died in 1904 whilst taking a cure in Baaden-weiler in Germany. He had been desperately ill, coughing up blood for days, and medicine was having no effect. Sensing he was dying, he asked for a bottle of champagne, sipped a glass, lay on his side and died. How charming. Optimistic to the end, he had written to his mother a few days earlier saying he'd booked his passage on a steamer to return home.

News of his death soon spread throughout Russia, and the nation mourned. Many remembering how his humour and compassion had helped them to cope with their often harsh lives, now gathered outside the station to pay their respects to their beloved Chekhonte. Unfortunately his coffin had been loaded onto a goods wagon carrying frozen oysters, and when it arrived in Moscow, another funeral procession for a General Keller from Manchuria was also taking place – complete with military band, and Chekhov's mourners mistakenly followed the military band. Gorki was appalled. 'This is the way we treat our great writers!' But how Chekhov would have laughed, it was the sort of absurd scenario he might well have penned himself.

If reading this foreword and these short plays awakens in you a desire to read Chekhov's short stories, I will feel greatly rewarded. And believe me, dear readers – so will you!

* * *

There have been many good in-depth biographies written about Chekhov. May I recommend those of Ernest Simmons, Ronald Hingley, Donald Rayfield, Sophie Lafitte, William Gerhardie (who spent his early years in Russia,) and V.S. Pritchett. I have gained a great deal of information from them, and would like to express my gratitude.

I would also like to thank Luke Roberts, Alla Figoff, Ignat Avesey, and Ludmilla Matthews for their encouragement.

The Summer of the Eclipse was presented for a season by The Butterfly Prawn Company at The Baron's Court Theatre on the 25th March 1997, with the following cast:

NIKOLAI-ANDREICH	Silas Hawkins.
VARENKA	Taryn Dielle.
IRINA-IVANEVNA	Pippa Rathborne.
GENERAL KARELIN	Bryan Hands.
KOOZMA-MAXIMOVICH	Jason Pethers.
TATIANA	Laura Martin.

The play was directed by Elizabeth Gamberoni.
Co-Director Bryan Hands.
Costume Co-ordinator and Set Design by Luke Pascoe.

———————————

The Dental Surgeon was presented by The Butterfly Prawn Company for a season on March 25th 1997, with the following cast:

KOORYATIN	Grant Davison.
VONMEGLAZOV	Guy Hemphill.
MASHA	Elizabeth Gamberoni.

Directed by Bryan Hands.
Co-Director Elizabeth Gamberoni.
Costume Co-ordinator and Set Design by Luke Pascoe.

"THE SUMMER OF THE ECLIPSE"

from

"Notes from the Journal of a Quick-tempered Man."

by

Anton Chekhov.

Translated and freely adapted by Elizabeth Gamberoni.

"THE SUMMER OF THE ECLIPSE"

Description of the characters

NIKOLAI-ANDREICH:	A bachelor in his late thirties. He is extremely pedantic, and somewhat humourless. A word will sometimes take his fancy and he will pronounce it lovingly, syllable by syllable.
VARENKA:	An attractive widow in her early thirties, desperate to remarry. She cannot pronounce her R's.
IRINIA-IVANEVNA:	(Varenka's mother) An attractive woman, equally determined to marry Varenka off.
GENERAL KARELIN:	A crusty old man with a good sense of humour, occasionally sentimental. A randy old sod.
KOOZMA-MAXIMOVICH:	A Captain – retired from the Army due to war wounds. In his early thirties. He has an awkward limp, and occasional spasms of stuttering (to be used at the actor's discretion). He speaks with a Hooray Henry accent which is quite natural to him. Might wear a monocle. (When were they invented?) He has a high-pitched laugh.
TATIANA:	In her late twenties. Unmarried. She is a guest at Varenka's home. She is very tall, clumsy, inclined to be hoydenish. Not very pretty, since Irina wouldn't want anyone staying who would compete with her daughter.

Scene One

It is a sunny day in the country and bird song can be heard. NIKOLAI-ANDREYEVICH *is seated on the balcony at the back of his house, which overlooks his garden, and that of his neighbour* IRINA-IVANEVNA. *He is filling in his journal*

NIKOLAI: Ah the cuckoo. [*He listens, takes a deep breath and exhales, then leans forward and addresses the audience*] I am a serious person – an Accountant by profession, in my mature years. I am of an [*searches for the right word*] – academic nature, ever eager to expand my not in-con-sid-erable knowledge on a multiplicity of subjects, on which – purely for my own pleasure, I write dissertations. Indeed this summer I am studying Fiscal Law. [*modest chuckle*] WHICH, for the unenlightened means Law pertaining to the public revenue – the ex-cheq-u-er! I am currently writing a thesis entitled: "The Dog-Tax: Its Past and Future!" [*primly*] As you may well imagine, I am a man little interested in such trivialities as young ladies – w-women, love songs, the moon, and such like nonsense. I like order in my life. I do NOT like putting off until tomorrow that which should be done today. However lately ... unfortunately ... [*His mind drifts*] Dear me – what was I doing? Ah yes! My journal ... Where was I up to? [*He picks up his diary and reads out*] Today, Wed-nes-day the 4th of August, in the year of our Lord 1887. Punctually at 10 o'clock this morning, dear Maman poured my coffee, and now that I have consumed it, I have come onto my balcony to resume working on "The Dog-Tax: Its Past and Future". [*He picks up his quill, then replaces it*] My balcony overlooks my garden and those of my neighbours. New residents have occupied the dachas on either side, alas since dear Maman and myself passed a peaceful season here last summer, and unfortunately a great many social occasions are now taking place. The dacha to my right has been rented for the season by Captain Koozma-Maximovitch Galchino – prematurely retired from the Army, due to injuries he suffered whilst fighting a gallant rearguard action in the last war; when he sustained one bullet wound in the left hip, and another in the right temple. And the dacha to my left has been purchased by Madame Irina-Ivanevna, oh-er what's her name, where she resides with her widowed daughter Nadenka ... or is it Mashenka? – however that is irrelevant, a lady of some [*He swallows*] attraction ... Varenka perhaps??? No matter! Oh dear!! [*He dabs his brow*] I really must continue my thesis. Now where are my notes? ... [*He locates them and reads out*] Historical Survey. "Judging from certain passing references to be found in Herodotus and Xenophon, the dog-tax arose from ... [*He stiffens as he hears "Tra-la-la-ing" coming from the garden to his left. He averts his head and covers his brow with a hand*]

VARENKA *enters her garden. She is wearing a floral-sprigged gown, and pretends she is looking for something. She casts a surreptitious glance in* NIKOLAI*'s direction, smoothes back her hair, plucks a flower, and continues "La-la-la-ing"*

NIKOLAI *peers at her through a crack in his fingers*

NIKOLAI: THAT – is Nadenka – or is it Mashenka? No matter. She is PRETENDING not to have seen me.

Getting no reaction from NIKOLAI, VARENKA *bursts into impassioned song*

VARENKA: Dost thou wecall that mel-o-deee, so foool, so foool of berleeeeess.

Dost thou wecall that foun-tain small, where we exchanged a keeeeess.

NIKOLAI: I shall feign not to have noticed her.

VARENKA [*melodramatically starts back*]: Oh, Nikolai-Andweich, I didn't see you. How you startled me. [*claps a hand to her breast*] Good morning.

NIKOLAI [*mutters*]: Good morning Mashenka.

VARENKA: VAWENKA! Oh Nicolas I am SO upset. I must have lost a bauble from my bwacelet when we stwolled in the garden last evening, admiwing the wed woses and the sunset.

NIKOLAI: Oh ... my word ... what a pity.

VARENKA: I wonder if you could spare me a few moments to help me search for it?

NIKOLAI [*stiffly*]: Well – as you know, I AM working on this very important thesis, "The Dog-Tax: Its Past ... "

VARENKA [*hurriedly interrupts*]: Of course, of course ... Fascinating!!! [*sighs*] Oh dear! I shall never be able to find it all by my little self.

NIKOLAI: I shall of course come to your assistance, if you will just allow me to complete this ph-phrase. One must not damn up inspiration when it is in full flow, Nadenka.

VARENKA: Vawenka!!! Of course not.

NIKOLAI: I'll j-just finish this sentence, then join you tout-de suite.

VARENKA: Thank you Nicolas. Such a Sir Galahad! I'll be waiting by the gweenhouse. [*She delicately sniffs the flower she is holding, then crosses the stage, singing*]
Dost thou wecall that foun-tain small where we exchanged a keeeeess.

NIKOLAI [*terror-stricken*]: Oh dear! That means she'll take my arm. [*He frantically mops his brow*]

With a last lingering glance at NIKOLAI, VARENKA *waggles her fingers in his direction and calls out*

VARENKA: A tout à l'heure then Nicolas. [*She exits*]

NIKOLAI [*shakily*]: Oh my word ... that means she'll take my arm again. Whenever a young lady for some reason takes my arm, I always feel like a hook, on which someone has hung a large voluptuous fur coat. The last time I escorted Nadenka ... or is it Mashenka? she ... she ... "pressed" herself against me. [*He breathes shakily*] Between ourselves, she has rather a passionate nature – her Grandfather was Armenian you know, and she is gifted with a way of holding your arm, with the full weight of her w-w-well-proportioned b-body. Attaching herself to one like a leech. Last evening her mother Irina-Ivanevna held a soirée, and later we all went down to the river to hear the peasants singing. On the way there we passed General Karelin's estate, and his massive dog barked in a most aggressive manner, and then it leapt at the gate, and Varenka – or is it Nadenka, pressed still closer to me. [*sadly*] Then the dog barked again and it reminded me of my still incomplete thesis, "The Dog-Tax: Its Past and Future," and I couldn't enjoy the choir at all.

VARENKA [*screams offstage*]: Oh Nikolai-Andweich – please come quickly. I'm frightened.

NIKOLAI [*leaps to his feet*]: What is it?

VARENKA [*pokes her head around the corner*]: There's a fwog on the cwazy paving, and I dare not pass it. I'm tewified of fwogs.

NIKOLAI: I shall be with you immediately.

VARENKA [*demurely*]: I'll be by the gweenhouse door [*She exits*]

NIKOLAI [*decisively sits down*] [*To himself*]: No. NO!!! Dammit I cannot go on having my time consumed in this way. They will find out I am a man of quick temper, a very quick-tempered fellow indeed when you intrude on my studies.

VARENKA [*calls from offstage*]: Nikolai-Andweich.

NIKOLAI [*sighs*]: I'm coming. I'm coming.

Blackout

End of Scene One

Scene Two

A lively polka is played for some second, before the lights slowly come up. It is morning. NIKOLAI *is seated as before on his balcony making an entry in his journal*

NIKOLAI: Friday the 6th of August 1887. [*He sighs and addresses the audience*] Regrettably I have made little progress with my thesis. So many social goings-on. All of them time consuming. Last evening Count Kooznetski held a ball, to which everyone of socially acceptable status was invited. A large number of Officers attended from the Count's former Regiment which is stationed nearby for summer manoeuvres – SO, there was much giggling and flirting from all the young ladies present. But, by adhering rigidly to dear Maman's side, I managed to escape most of the dancing. However Varenka – or is it Nadenka, DID manage to inveigle me into a waltz before the evening was at an end. [*tuts*] I am in the deuce of a predicament with her. She seems to have got it into her head that I'm in love with her – which I'm not! She professes NOT to return this love – which I don't feel anyway. And because of this she overwhelms me with unjustified, and unwanted compassion – ministering to my "wounded soul". God bless me! [*mops his brow*] Last evening she WHIRLED me out of the ballroom onto the veranda, and there she . . . she . . . [*swallows*] "p-pressed" herself against me. She stared at me with those enormous dark eyes and sighed . . . [*dreamily*] eyes like black velvet. [*He leans confidentially towards the audience*] Her Grandfather WAS Armenian you know. Then she squeezed my arm again, and said "I am so sorry to inflict such suffering on you, but alack! My heart was given to another and went with him to the tomb." Then she sighed again and pressed herself against my chest. At which precise moment, fortuitously, others came onto the veranda to take the air, and PLEADING, that I did not wish to be the cause of her losing her hitherto unbesmirched name, I was thus able to drag her back inside, where, to my INTENSE relief, dear Maman came up to claim me, pleaded a headache, and we were able to drive home forthwith. [*He delicately dabs his brow, remembering his near escape*]

Whoops and shouts of laughter from both men and women can be heard coming from the next garden

NIKOLAI *turns his head in the direction of the noise*

NIKOLAI: I have been invited to join them again today, but I shall not go. I shall NOT go. I – WILL – RESIST!!! [*He laughs shortly*] Ha ha! They will find I am a man of iron will, whom it is better NOT to provoke. A man who might not be responsible for his actions if he is dragged from his cogitations. I have work to do for posterity! NO! They would do better NOT to meddle with a quick-tempered fellow like myself.

He decisively squares his shoulders, dips his quill in the ink, and commences writing

GENERAL KARELIN *comes into* VARENKA *'s garden. He crosses the stage slowly, leaning on a cane: occasionally he pauses to dig the cane into a flower bed. He mutters to himself*

GENERAL: The garden isn't looking as good as it did last year, when the Krilov's had it. No, I'm damned if it is. Huh! Chickweed! [*He walks on a few paces and suddenly notices* NIKOLAI *sitting on his balcony*]

NIKOLAI *spies* THE GENERAL, *covers his brow with a hand and continues busily writing, occasionally glancing at* THE GENERAL *through a crack in his fingers*

GENERAL [*calls up*]: Ah good morning, Nikolai-Andreyevitch.

NIKOLAI: Good morning General Karelin.

GENERAL: Beautiful day!

NIKOLAI [*through clenched teeth*]: Yes. Beautiful.

GENERAL: Enjoy yourself at the Ball last evening did you? My word there were some ravishing young demoiselles there. Beautiful!!! Made me wish I were twenty years younger. [*gives a dirty chuckle*] Made even my old heart tumble.

NIKOLAI *pulls a disapproving face, but makes no reply*

GENERAL: Didn't see you dancin' much. I was never off the floor in my young days. Couldn't have kept me off the floor last night if it hadn't been for me gout. Could have shown them would-be gallants a step or two. I can tell you! [*sighs*] That I could ... [*He prods at something with his cane*] [*mutters*] Crabgrass! [*looks up again at* NIKOLAI] Thought you were supposed to be joinin' us today?

NIKOLAI: I'm afraid that will NOT be possible. I am behind with my research.

GENERAL: Oh yes? What is it you're working on?

NIKOLAI [*visibly brightens*]: I'm studying Fiscal Law and writing a thesis on ...

GENERAL [*hastily interrupts*]: Yes! Yesyesyes! I remember you talking about it the other day. [*slight pause*] Mind you I don't blame you for lyin' doggo, keeping out of harm's reach. [*He points over his shoulder with his cane*] Irina-Ivanevna's got everyone over there preparing some GHASTLY berries for jam making. They're all sittin' out on the veranda with huge bowlfuls of cherries and some other damned fruit, and she's armed each of them with a vicious lookin' hairpin to get the stones out. [*chuckles*] I made me escape. Mind you Nikolai-Andreich, there are SOME benefits to be derived from old age. As I always say, everything has its positive side – there's no one can force you to do what you don't want to. [*chuckles drily*] Yeees, getting into the sere and yellow does have some consolations. [*He sighs, then adds disgruntedly*] Precious damned few! [*sighs again*] Ah well – I'll just take a turn round the garden and leave you in peace. [*He turns away, walks a few paces, then turns again in* NIKOLAI*'s direction*] Me memory's goin' a bit. What did you say that thesis of yours was called?

NIKOLAI [*enthusiastically*]: The Dog-Tax: Its Past and Future. [*quickly*] References ARE to be found in Herodotus and Xenophon ...

GENERAL [*brusquely interrupts*]: Ah yes! Yesyesyesyes! All comes back to me now. You spoke of it the other evening I recall.

[*He continues on his way*] [*mutters to himself*] In quite some tedious detail.

NIKOLAI *once again immerses himself in his thesis*

THE GENERAL *walks on, pauses, and studies the sky. He follows the flight of a bird*

GENERAL [*mutters*]: It's gonna rain tomorrow. [*he takes out his pocket watch and studies it*] Devil's teeth! Still another hour to kill till lunch.

IRINA-IVANEVNA *comes on stage. She anxiously scans the garden till she sights* THE GENERAL

IRINA: Ah, THERE you are, General. I wondered WHERE you'd got to. [*She crosses to join him. Her manner towards him is slightly flirtatious*] Admiring the garden I see. I don't know whether you were acquainted with the former tenants, the Krilovs – but they let the garden go to an absolute waste! You cannot imagine! It's taken an army of men to put it to rights. [*coos*] I'm so glad I've got you on your own at last. I've been wanting to ask your advice, [*titters*] – on matters horticultural, having seen your magnificent estate. Erm – and by the way, Vladimir-Sergeyevitch, although I never had the pleasure of meeting your charming wife, I'm sure that now she is gone ... [*She glances sadly heavenwards*]

THE GENERAL *scowls, and irritably strides on*

IRINA *runs and catches him up*

IRINA: Now that she is gone ... I expect you must feel lonely. Please consider my home as your own, and call in whenever it ... [*She catches sight of* NIKOLAI] Nikolai-Andreyevitch There you are!!! We were expecting you hours ago – the girls were wondering WHERE you'd got to. [*She wags her folded fan at him and tries to conceal her disapproval with a smile*] Naughty boy!

NIKOLAI: Oh ... er, yes, er ... Good morning, Irina-Ivanevna.

IRINA: But what are you doing up there on your balcony all alone?

NIKOLAI: I'm working on my thesis. 'The Dog-Tax: Its P ... '

24

IRINA [*interrupts with a brilliant but grim smile*]: YES! You did mention it. Fascinating!! [*to* THE GENERAL] Quelle intelligence. Such erudition!

THE GENERAL *just humphs*

IRINA [*to* NIKOLAI]: Well leave it for the moment, my angel. All work and no play will make Nikolai a dull boy. Now come along! [*She beckons to him, turns, and continues walking arm in arm with* THE GENERAL] Such a hot day. Could I tempt you to a glass of kvass?

THE GENERAL *'s expression does not express enthusiasm*

GENERAL: Kvass??

IRINA: Kvass or LEMONADE? . . . a tot of vodka perhaps?

THE GENERAL *'s eyes brighten, his pace quickens, and he hobbles offstage with some alacrity, with* IRINA *by his side*

NIKOLAI: Damnit I will NOT permit people to talk to me as though I were a little boy. They will find out! I am a quick-tempered fellow, and woe betide anyone who plays games with me. If you drag me from my studies, then I won't be responsible for what happens. [*He angrily scribbles a few words*] They'd better watch out! [*He blots the word he has just written*]

VARENKA *'s voice coos from offstage*

VARENKA: Nikolai . . . Nikitoushka.

TATIANA [*voice offstage*]: Wait for me Koozma-Maximovitch.

KOOZMA *enters. He has an awkward comical gait, shooting one leg out to the side. His accent is affected, but natural to him and he wears a monocle*

KOOZMA [*calls out*]: I've tracked down one of them, ladies. Come along Nikolai, we cannot have f-f-fellows d-d-deserting their posts. Dammit man, we need reinforcements. [*He whinnies a laugh at his own joke*]

TATIANA *trills a laugh for far longer than the sally merits*

TATIANA: Oh, Koozma – you are a wit. Do hurry up Nikolai –

we're having such fun. Oh but you look so serious. What EVER is the matter?

VARENKA *appears, whispers tragically to* TATIANA

VARENKA: I KNOW what is the matter. I'll see to him. You two go on and find the others.

TATIANA *grabs hold of* KOOZMA*'s arm, practically yanking him off his feet. They exit*

VARENKA [*gently*]: Oh Nicolas – so sad and lonely you look up there. I know how you must be suffering. But you must not be on your own, pain is eased in company.

NIKOLAI, *embarrassed, makes no reply*

VARENKA: What would you say if the girl whom you love were to offer you eternal fwendship?

IRINA *appears behind* VARENKA*'s shoulders*

IRINA: Now COME ALONG Nicolai-Andreich.

NIKOLAI*'s shoulders slump*

NIKOLAI: I'm coming, I'm coming.

IRINA *exits, and with a last long backward glance,* VARENKA *follows her*

NIKOLAI: Oh this is too much! In the first place I am NOT in love with anyone, and in the second place, what on earth would I want with eternal friendship? [*He stands up*] Devil take it! [*He exits*]

Blackout

End of Scene Two

Scene Three

A lilting Russian folk song as the lights come slowly up. The general,
IRINA *and* VARENKA, *are seated at a large wooden table in the garden.*
Facing them sit KOOZMA *and* TATIANA
THE GENERAL *tosses back his vodka, then moodily surveys the wooden*
bowls facing him

GENERAL: You've stoned enough fruit there to feed an army.

IRINA: I shall let you have some of it when it's made. It's from an
   old Ukranian recipe of my Grand-mother's. It contains
   almost a bottle of cognac – should suit your palate.
   Vladimir-Sergeyevitch.

THE GENERAL *chuckles.* NIKOLAI *wanders onstage reading a book*

KOOZMA: What shall we do with the h-h-hairpins, Irina-Ivanevna,
   they're somewhat s-s-sticky.

IRINA: Leave them there for the time being. [*slightly irritable*]
   Where HAS Nikolai-Andreyevitch got himself to now,
   Varenka?

VARENKA: He's over by the cedar, Maman, studying a book on
   the eclipse of the sun.

GENERAL: Ah yes! The eclipse! Takes place tomorrow, doesn't
   it?

TATIANA [*giggles*]: Nikolai's always got his nose buried in a
   book.

IRINA [*indulgently*]: Quelle intelligence!

KOOZMA: I – er, think I'll go and join him. I need s-s-some of his
   literary advice on the work I myself am engaged on. [*He*
   picks up a very large folio from the table and hobbles in NIKOLAI *'s*
   direction]

TATIANA *races after him and grabs hold of his arm*

TATIANA: Oh DO let me come with you Koozma-Maximovitch. I
   am SO interested in literature and the Arts.

KOOZMA [*firmly*]: NO Tatiana. I would prefer to speak to Nikolai alone. The m-matter on which I w-wish to consult him is of a m-m-masculine nature, that would bore a delicate butter-fly like yourself.

TATIANA: Just as you say, Koozma. [*She curls a finger around a loose tendril of hair*] But don't be gone too long. [*With a last backward glance, she returns to the table*]

As KOOZMA *approaches,* NIKOLAI *scowls, and mutters to himself*

NIKOLAI: Hell's teeth. Never a damned moment's peace! [*He buries his face in his book*]

short pause

KOOZMA: I wonder c-c-could I disturb you Nikolai-Andreich I need your advice. I was m-m-most interested when you were discussing your dissertation the other day. "The Dog-Tax: Its Pap-past and F-future." Gripping stuff! You have a veritable gift for words, Nikolai. I was e-e-enthralled. [NIKO-LAI *adopts a suitably modest expression and leans back in his chair*] You s-s-see I too have literary aspirations, and had intended devoting my time to them this summer. [*sighs*] But, well as you know, w-w-what with the variegated dam-sels, and all the s-s-social functions going on, there has been little time. I d-do resolutely try to set about this honourable t-task each morning, but s-s-somehow, some-one always appears beneath my b-balcony and c-c-carries me off. So I have come to you – the M-Master, for some help. It would be m-most gracious if you could s-s-spare me some m-moments of your valuable time.

NIKOLAI [*expansively*]: Oh my dear boy – think nothing of it. Pray be seated.

KOOZMA *arranges his leg in a comfortable position and seats himself*

NIKOLAI: Now tell me, what is this lit-er-ary task you have set yourself?

KOOZMA [*intensely*]: I am wr-wr-writing my memoirs – the m-m-memoirs of a military man.

NIKOLAI [*gravely*]: Personal reminiscences – that's a good start. And what are you calling it?

KOOZMA: If you would allow me to read from it S-Sir, it wouldn't take t-t-too much of your time.

NIKOLAI *graciously nods, and* KOOZMA *staggers to his feet and unfolds his large portfolio. He clears his throat and reads out*

KOOZMA: The Memoirs of a C-C-Cavalry Officer.

NIKOLAI *gravely nods his head in approval of the title*

KOOZMA [*takes a deep breath and reads on*]: I was b-born in ...

TATIANA [*interrupt together*]: Koozma-Maximovitch.
VARENKA   : Nicolas.

IRINA [*hiding her irritation*]: Come along dear boys. We cannot have you two men of letters depriving us of your stimulating conversation.

GENERAL [*casts his eyes to heaven*]: Huh!

IRINA: Come and join us.

NIKOLAI *bestows a hostile glance in their direction and courteously gestures to* KOOZMA *to continue*

NIKOLAI: Pray continue, Koozma-Maximovitch.

KOOZMA: Well – er, th-that's as far as I've got, Sir.

NIKOLAI *blinks three times, mulls the sentence over*

NIKOLAI: I was born in ... yes, YES! The phrase DOES have a certain ... [*gesticulates*] – elegance.

IRINA [*claps her hands*]: Really, you Literati – that is enough!

TATIANA *rushes over, seizes* KOOZMA *by the arm, and practically yanks him off his feet*

NIKOLAI: We will discuss it another time, Koozma-Maximovitch. [*He crosses to the ladies*] Well I'm afraid I must be off. I am already a little en retard for lunch.

TATIANA: Aren't you lunching here?

VARENKA: But you promised us, Nikolai-Andweich. Last evening – don't you remember? [*stamps her foot*] You pwomised!

NIKOLAI: Well – er, I do apologise about that, but, er – you see, there IS poor Maman to consider. Our maid SHOULD have come to call me when lunch was ready. I shall have to have a word with her about that.

IRINA [*cautiously*]: Well – er, she DID come, Nikitoushka and I went back with her to see your poor dear Maman. Your mother WAS invited to lunch too you know, but she begs to be excused – she is a little fatigued after last evening. Well, she IS getting on in years now. She's lying down, Nikolai, and SPECIALLY requested that you should NOT disturb her.

VARENKA: Oh Maman!!! Nicolas wouldn't be so selfish as to do that. Would you Nicolas?

NIKOLAI *is lost for words*

GENERAL [*looks pointedly at his watch*]: Well now that that's all sorted out, perhaps we can get on with lunch.

IRINA: It should be ready at any moment now, Vladimir-Sergeitch. Meanwhile DO help yourself to another vodka.

THE GENERAL *helps himself to a vodka and knocks it back*

IRINA: Come children – help me clear the bowls. And you, Koozma dear boy. Come along!

The three women gather up the bowls and exit, followed, reluctantly, by KOOZMA. NIKOLAI *disgruntedly seats himself at the wooden table*

GENERAL: Like a nip of vodka?

NIKOLAI [*coldly*]: Thank you, no. I rarely touch it.

GENERAL: Huh! More fool you. [*He pours himself a glass and tosses it back*]

long silence

GENERAL: Dined here before, have you?

NIKOLAI [*coolly*]: No. Not as yet.

GENERAL: Well I can vouch for the fodder. Excellent. Excellent!!! I did a recce around the kitchen a little earlier. [*He counts off on his fingers*] We've got cold soup, tongue with boiled peas, roast chicken and stewed fruit. Mmmm! I can smell it from here already. Delicious! [*confidentially*] But do yourself a favour, lad. DON'T sit next to that Koozma-Maximovitch fella – he'll put you orff your fodder. His jaws are inclined to [*He demonstrates*] – seize up on occasions – due I believe to that wound he sustained in his head. [*muses*] He eats rather as if he's got a bit between his teeth. Yes! Quite un-nervin' dammit. Stammers sometimes too, have you noticed? And he never stops rollin' his bread into little balls – don't know whether that's because of his wound, or to stop that Tatiana gel grabbin' hold of his arm. I was watchin' her yesterday – she very nigh yanked the damned thing orff. What she lacks in beauty she certainly makes up for in strength – eh what Nikolai? [*He chortles at his own joke*] Mind you, between you and me, I don't think Irina encourages too many beauties to call – certainly not the younger ones, doesn't want too much competition for her Varenka, does she? NOT till she's got her safely orff her hands again. [*He sniffs again*] Mmmm Delicious!!! Dear God, how much longer do we have to wait for lunch? I think I'll go and find out what's happenin' – IF I don't get waylaid en route. The gong should be goin' soon, and I can't move as quickly as I used to. [*He hobbles offstage*]

NIKOLAI *sighs, and buries his face disgruntedly in his book*

VARENKA *trips onstage.* NIKOLAI *glances up, and* VARENKA *melodramatically starts back*

VARENKA: Oh Nikolai – I didn't know you were here.

NIKOLAI *feigns interest in his book, and* VARENKA *seats herself beside him on the bench. Getting no reaction, she slides a little closer.* NIKOLAI, *embarrassed, gives vent to a deep sigh*

VARENKA: Why are you sighing? [*She herself gives a heartfelt sigh*] Ah I KNOW why you are sighing. You love someone – that's what it is. But in the name of our fwendship, I BEG you to believe that the woman whom you love holds you in the vewy gweatest of wespect. [*sadly*] She cannot answer your affection with like, but is the fault hers? If her heart for so long belonged to another and went with him to the tomb? [*She gives a long shivering sigh*] I too have suffered.

A gong sounds in the distance, and NIKOLAI *leaps to his feet with some relief.* VARENKA *grabs his arm and pulls him back on the bench with one quick tug. She delicately mops her eyes with a lace handkerchief and pats* NIKOLAI*'s hand*

THE GENERAL, *arm in arm with* IRINA, *appears behind them, heading towards the house.* IRINA *restrains* THE GENERAL, *who is ravenously hungry.* IRINA *smiles indulgently at the young couple, who are seated in front of them. She smiles up at* THE GENERAL

IRINA: Ah youth, youth! [*She pats* THE GENERAL*'s hand with her fan*] Of course, Varenka's only the teeniest slip of a girl. [*laughs gaily*] I was barely more than a babe in arms myself when I married for the first time. [*She smiles up at him*] Still, it's not THAT long ago that we can't remember. Is it mon chere General?

GENERAL [*noisily clears his throat*]: Herumph. Hmmm. Well! Better not put your excellent cook out of temper by allowing her food to get cold eh!.

IRINA [*sings out*]: Come along children.

Lights fade to a complete blackout

End of Scene Three

Scene Four

Soft balalaika music is heard playing. All the lights come up, NIKOLAI *nervously smoking, sits alone on the bench. He scribbles something in a notebook.* IRINA, *arm in arm with* THE GENERAL, *walk in his direction*

GENERAL: An excellent lunch, excellent! I must congratulate you. Superb cuisine!

IRINA [*laughs merrily*]: Ah, mon chere, Vladimir-Sergeitch – vous me flattez.

GENERAL: Pas du tout. The dinner the other evening was ALSO excellent I recall.

IRINA: Come come – it was nothing out of the ordinary, after all we weren't even expecting you.

GENERAL [*thoughtfully*]: That is what I thought. Which means a consistently high standard. [*He comes to a halt and kisses her hand lovingly*] Tell me Irina-Ivanevna ...

IRINA [*breathlessly*]: Yes, General?

GENERAL: This cook of yours Irina-Ivanevna, is she FROM the locality?

note to the actor – THE GENERAL *knows that with his enormous estate, and good reputation, he could easily prise a local cook from* IRINA

IRINA [*in her parisian ensemble – a teensie bit miffed*]: From the locality!!! Heavens no!! She's from Petersburgh! Been with me for years!! Travels the WORLD with us!!!

GENERAL [*disappointed*]: Oh I seeeee.

He and IRINA *seat themselves.* KOOZMA *comes onstage with* TATIANA *in hot pursuit. She tugs at his arm, practically yanking him off balance*

TATIANA: Did you think you'd lost me to that handsome Hussar, Koozma?

KOOZMA [*through clenched teeth*]: N-n-no!

NIKOLAI [*looks up from his notes as they join him*]: Where are all the others?

IRINA [*whispers to* THE GENERAL]: You know who HE'S missing don't you. [*she calls out*] Varvara ... Vareeeeenka my darling.

VARENKA [*appears clutching a butterfly net*]: Here I am, Maman.

IRINA: Nikolai-Andreich was asking after you.

NIKOLAI [*absent-mindedly looks up from his notes*]: And where are all the others?

VARENKA: They've gone down to the gwove to catch butterflies. I was just going to join them.

NIKOLAI: Pray don't do that.

VARENKA *abruptly seats herself next to him*

NIKOLAI: There are matters to discuss – important matters. I have decided pro tem to abandon my thesis, "The Dog-Tax: Its Past and Future."

GENERAL [*casts his eyes to heaven and mutters*]: God's teeth!

VARENKA [*tragically*]: Oh Nicolas!

KOOZMA: S-s-sorry to hear that, Sir.

NIKOLAI: I knew YOU would appreciate the sacrifice I am making. Koozma. Yes! I have decided to set it aside pro tem in the interests of posterity.

TATIANA [*whispering loudly to* KOOZMA]: What does pro tem mean?

KOOZMA: Shhhhh!

NIKOLAI: Tomorrow will be an historic date – the 7th of August 1887, on which a rare event takes place, an occasion of epoch making and scientific importance. To wit! The eclipse of the sun!!! I intend to monitor it and document my findings, and shall devote the remainder of my holiday to writing a dissertation based on my personal observations, which will, when completed, be forwarded to the ob-ser-va-tory in Petersburgh, AND, more importantly, to the Royal Ob-ser-va-tory in London's Greenwich – the most important centre of astronomical data in the entire hemi-sphere. [*He permits himself a brief smile*] This should ensure me a small place in the annals of astronomical history.

choruses of "Oohs" and "Ahs" from the ladies

KOOZMA: Well spoken, Sir.

NIKOLAI: As you may well imagine, it will be a Herculean task, and even *I* will be unable to tackle it single-handedly. I am therefore requesting the help of those of you here present, and the others when they return from butterflying, to assist me in this glorious work. Have I your consent?

Cries of assent from all, save THE GENERAL

Of course, of course. How thrilling! Isn't it excitin' – Varenka? etc. etc.

KOOZMA [*visibly moved*]: Nikolai-Andreyevitch, Sir. Since you – in the interests of science have so nobly set aside the P-past and F-future of the Dog-Tax, I will follow your selfless example, and postpone the completion of my Memoirs. For I would consider it an honour to work with you, Sir.

NIKOLAI [*touched*]: Thank-you Koozma-Maximovitch. [*The two men gravely shake hands*]

GENERAL: Ha!!!

TATIANA: Aren't you going to help too, General?

GENERAL: Shouldn't think anyone's assistance will be of much use tomorrow. It's gonna rain.

TATIANA: It's only old age which makes you so pessimistic. Vladimir-Sergeyevitch.

THE GENERAL *bestows a withering glance in her direction, and realising she has been tactless,* TATIANA *covers her mouth with her hands*

NIKOLAI: I have already sketched out a general plan of campaign, and will allot you each a task later when I have worked out the minor details. [*vaguely*] Nooooow ... [*His attention returns to his notes*]

GENERAL: I say, who are those people coming down the lane?

Everyone, save NIKOLAI, *watch the approaching group. Their heads gradually moving – this takes about 30 seconds*

As the by-passers get within recognisable distance, the faces of KOOZMA *and* THE GENERAL *light up.* THE GENERAL *strokes his moustache, and* KOOZMA *sits with his mouth wide open.* THE THREE WOMEN *watch the approaching group, stony-faced*

GENERAL [*in an aside to* KOOZMA]: I must say I envy those young Hussars accompanying such beauties, eh what? I seem to remember the petite demoiselle with her curling black hair – wasn't she at the Ball last evening?

KOOZMA [*tremulously*]: Yes, it's Nastasia-Timofeyevna.

GENERAL: Charmante! And the filly with her in the yellow silk dress?

KOOZMA: That's Anna-Nikolaevna.

GENERAL: Like a young spring flower – eh what, Koozma?

NIKOLAI *vaguely glances up*

IRINA [*icily*]: She's not as young as she might seem, Vladimir-Sergeyevitch.

VARENKA: She only SEEMS young because she's so bwainless.

TATIANA: Anyway, one of her shoulder blades sticks out.

NIKOLAI [*vaguely*]: Elegant though – must have bought that gown in Paris.

VARENKA: Elegant!!! I think she's a fwump!

NIKOLAI [*naifly*] Do you? [*Oblivious of her anger, he returns to his notes*]

As the party in the lane come abreast, they all wave. The two men beam back. KOOZMA *struggles to get his leg in position, stands, makes a military bow and clicks his heels.* THE GENERAL *tries to rise out of his chair, but can't quite manage it. He sinks back, draws in his stomach, and gives a jaunty salute. The three women, as though their mouths were attached to the same piece of string, switch on sudden, rigid, frigid smiles, and wave in a desultory fashion.* NIKOLAI, *oblivious of the tension, continues reading his notes. The eyes of the party follow the procession until it has disappeared from view*

KOOZMA [*sinks back in his seat, sighing*]: I was conversing with N-N-Nastasia-Timofeyevna last evening. Then I went to get her some l-l-lemonade, and when I returned, that BOUNDER accompanying her now, had dragged her off to dance the Mazurka. [*He sighs again*]

NIKOLAI [*vaguely*]: Yes, she is a pretty girl.

The three women try to get even

TATIANA: Weren't there some handsome beaux at the Ball last night, Varenka? My heavens, I danced so much I scarcely had time to draw breath.

IRINA: That charming Mr. Zhigalov that was paying you so much attention, Varenka, now I thought HE was good-looking.

VARENKA: No, I didn't think HE was good-looking, Maman, but I DID think he was attwactive.

TATIANA: And the Polish Count who partnered me in the Grand Rond, now I thought he was attractive. Mr. Bortsova would be quite good looking too, if his nose weren't quite so like a thimble.

The three women dissolve in giggles

TATIANA: And Boris-Martinovitch is such a wit, and isn't he a darling?

VARENKA: And he dances like a dweam.

IRINA [*laughs indulgently*]: Listen to the two children chattering away like magpies. Come, mes jolies filles why don't we assess the charms of the gallants we have with us. I'll take Koozma first of all. Now you, Koozma, are, as we all know, a dashing and courageous officer. BUT – you are NOT good looking; however you ARE attractive.

KOOZMA *self-consciously smiles*

TATIANA: What about the General?

IRINA: Ah, the General is in a class by himself – full of charm and wit, a veritable heartbreaker.

It is obvious from THE GENERAL*'s expression of self-satisfaction, that he agrees with* IRINA

TATIANA: And Nikolai?

IRINA: Now you, Monsieur Nicolas, are NOT good looking, but you are – "quite" attractive. [*consolingly*] How CAN one describe you. You have an ... [*searches for the word*] an – "interesting" face. [*She sighs*] But the most important thing in a man is NOT his looks, but his brain. Isn't that so, Varenka?

VARENKA *sighs and casts her eyes demurely down*

IRINA: Tatiana, Koozma, come along. We have to get the baskets. And if you like to come up to the house dear General, I'll see that you have some tea.

NIKOLAI, *already mortified with embarrassment, becomes even more so as the others depart, leaving him alone with* VARENKA. IRINA *walks a few paces, then trips back and whispers to* NIKOLAI

IRINA: You must not be too downcast, Nicolas, for if you KEEP persevering, it is your spiritual qualities that will win the day in the end. [*She exits*] Courage mon brave.

NIKOLAI: Well – I, er, really have to be going – I have my plan to prepare for the eclipse, and anyway, dear Maman will be wondering what has become of me.

VARENKA: Oh you WOULDN'T be so cwuel as to disturb her. And in any case you can't go now, it's all awanged. We're all going to the woods, and you're to help me.

NIKOLAI [*terror stricken*]: The w-w-woods. W-what for?

VARENKA [*gives him a long languorous look*]: To pick mush-wooms.

NIKOLAI: Oh!

long silence

VARENKA *slides along the bench till her arm is touching his*

VARENKA: Tell me, Monsieur Nicolas, why is your face so sad? Why do you not speak?

NIKOLAI [*swallows convulsively*]: W-what would you l-like me to say? Nadenka?

38

VARENKA: Vawenka!! Please, do say something.

NIKOLAI: What about?

VARENKA: Well – something you think might – interest me.

He searches for something to say

NIKOLAI: Well – er, the felling of f-forests in Russia is causing enormous havoc – deforestation.

VARENKA*'s face stiffens. She assumes a gentler expression and sighs*

VARENKA: Ah Nicolas, I see you are avoiding a heart to heart. [*long silence*] It is as if you wish to punish me with your silence. Your emotion is unwequited and you wish to suffer in solitude and in silence. It's awful, Nicolas. [*Further long silence*]

VARENKA: Won't you accept this hand of fwendship?

She takes his hand and presses it against her thigh. NIKOLAI *attempts to withdraw it, but she places her other hand on top, firmly imprisoning his.* NIKOLAI *stares straight ahead, as though paralysed. A further long silence ensues*

VARENKA [*also looking straight ahead*]: He does not answer. He obviously wants me to make a sacwifice. But how CAN I love him, if my heart still belongs to another, and went with him to the tomb? And yet . . . and yet, I'll think about it . . . I shall summon up all the spiwitual wesources at my command, and perhaps – even at the price of my own happiness, deliver him fwom his suffewing.

TATIANA *dashes on, clutching a basket*

TATIANA: Do come on you two slow coaches – we're waiting.

IRINA *races on after her*

IRINA: What nonsense you do talk, Tatiana. There's no rush. We have all afternoon. [*hisses*] Silly girl! Come away.

But the damage has been done, and NIKOLAI *leaps up and hooks his arms through* IRINA*'s and* TATIANA*'s*

NIKOLAI: If I'm to come, we shall have to set off now, or I will not have time, for I have a great deal of work to do this evening, and do remember, tomorrow we must make an early start.

They exit, leaving VARENKA *alone*

VARENKA: Oh weally! Stupid girl.

End of Scene Four

Scene Five

Sad Russian folksong to be heard in the background. Lights slowly come up. It is morning and NIKOLAI *is seated on his balcony. He finishes writing a sentence, blots it, looks around him and sighs*

NIKOLAI: Typical summer weather. Which means the temperature's well below freezing point, a cold biting wind, rain, mud, and a smell of mothballs caused by Maman dragging all her heavy winter coats out of the chests, which has brought on my asthma. [*He pulls a shawl around his shoulders*] An absolutely FOUL morning! It is – to be precise, the 7th August, the day of the eclipse. I finalised my preparations for it during the night, because ... because I ... couldn't sleep. I shall definitely delay my appearance to Irina-Ivanevna's ... Apropos of which, I earlier received a letter from Mashenka – or is it Nadenka, delivered by her maid, requesting that I meet her in the summerhouse beforehand ... [*sighs tremulously*] My heart is thumping again ... I shall NOT go to the summerhouse. Perhaps that isn't polite, but she could hardly expect me to go in this downpour – could she???? [*He draws the shawl close round his shoulders*] Yesterday – when we were out mushrooming, I suddenly found the two of us quite alone, and Mashenka whispered to me, "I have something to tell you. Don't follow the others". I had a nasty foreboding, but waited out of a sense of decorum, and then she t-took my arm, and led me off somewhere down an avenue of trees. Her whole being expressed inner conflict, she was pale, and breathing heavily, and her eyes were enormous. [*shakily*] ... eyes like b-black velvet. Then she murmured, "I want to tell you – NO! I can't, I can't ... " THEN ... I could see, that she HAD made her mind up, for those black eyes flashed – her grandfather WAS Armenian you know – then she ... [*He trembles*] p-pressed herself against my chest – her heart was beating wildly – or was it mine? Then she suddenly sprang back – "Someone's coming", she whispered. "Meet me in the summerhouse tomorrow morning, before the eclipse of the sun". And OFF she went. [*mops his brow*] Completely at a loss, with my heart palpitating terribly, I made my way home. There, "The Past and the Future of the Dog-Tax" awaited me, but somehow, well, it didn't seem so important. [*pause*] I was furious!! I would even go so far as to say I was fearsome in my wrath. I'm quick-tempered damnit, and woe betide anyone who plays games with me, and when the maid came to call me for supper, I yelled at her – "Get out!" Such wrath bodes ill. [*He draws on his cigarette*] [*disgruntled*] I could eat no supper. I sat on the balcony trying to force myself to work, but inspiration would not come. It was a dreadful evening!! Darkness fell at last, and a revolting moon crept up from behind the scented shrubbery. The air was still with an unpleasant smell of new mown hay, and ... and ... somewhere a balalaika played and voices sang sad sweet songs of love ... and ... a picture of Mashenka floated before me ... Devil's teeth!! I cannot have such trivialities coming between me and my philosophical studies. I shall make it clear to her today, that I will. I will NOT behave like a moonstruck youth! [*He mournfully draws out his watch, gazes at it, then glances up at the sky. Suddenly a broad smile lights up his whole countenance*] It's stopped! It's stopped raining!!! [*excitedly*] Now have I got everything? The smoked glass – yes! The sketching pads and pencils, ah – here they are. A compass – yes, ... where are my dark glasses and ...

TATIANA *and* KOOZMA *appear in the next garden*

TATIANA: There he is – he probably overslept.

KOOZMA [*calls up, puzzled*]: Aren't you coming Nikolai-Andreich.

NIKOLAI [*cheerily*]: Of course, of course. Just checking on my equipment.

TATIANA [*sullenly*]: Very kind of you to deign to turn up at last, I'm sure. It was still pitch dark when I got up. Nightingales singing, not larks.

KOOZMA [*irritably*]: Oh v-v-very droll!

Oblivious of TATIANA*'s ill-humour,* NIKOLAI *continues packing things into his gladstone bag*

NIKOLAI: ... compass ... Did you manage to get any more volunteers, Koozma?

KOOZMA [*dreamily*]: Oh yes, yes. Nastasia-Timofeyevna's arrived with Anna-Ivanevna ...

TATIANA [*interrupts*]: And a handsome Captain from the Hussars, with a friend, but I don't suppose Koozma even noticed them.

NIKOLAI [*vaguely*]: Good ... good ... That's splendid news ... notebook ... I'm glad everyone realises the importance of the occasion. I'll just put on my goloshes and join you post haste. [*He exits*]

TATIANA: It's too ridiculous! Nikolai insisted we should be punctual, and now he's kept everyone waiting. It's really too boring.

KOOZMA: I'd b-better make sure the girls have got their smoked glass, and s-suchlike.

TATIANA: I'll come with you. [*She goes to take his arm, but he shakes her off*] I could think of lots more exciting things to do than this.

KOOZMA: Well, j-jollywell go and do them then, and s-s-stop grumbling and spoiling it for everyone else.

IRINA [*comes on-stage and calls out*]: Just you two? Where's Varenka?

TATIANA: She was going to the summerhouse when I last saw her. [*mutters*] Of course it was so dark, it could've been a ghost I suppose.

IRINA [*incredulously*]: The summerhouse???

TATIANA [*snaps*]: Oh Irina-Ivanevna, that was hours ago.

They cross to join her. The sound of jingling bridle can be heard offstage

IRINA: Good heavens! That's the General's brougham. [*She chuckles*] Strictly entre nous, I didn't expect the General to take part, and certainly not in SUCH weather.

VARENKA *comes onstage and gazes over at* NIKOLAI *'s empty balcony*

IRINA: Oh Varenka, there you are. [*gazes into her face*] You look very pale child. Is anything wrong? Ah, here's Nikolai – at last!!

NIKOLAI *enters, laden with equipment, wearing goloshes. He beams round at everyone*

NIKOLAI: Ah, good morning, good morning dear friends – or should I say, colleagues. [*He casts a timid glance at* VARENKA] Good-morning Mashenka.

IRINA: Varenka!

VARENKA *stiffly inclines her head, but makes no reply* – KOOZMA *places his bag on the table*

NIKOLAI: Koozma, dear fellow. I have revised the plans we were discussing yesterday. I MYSELF will now measure the diameter of the sun and moon, and since you informed me that you are a gifted artist, it will be your responsibility to sketch in the Corona. The General can measure the temperature, and I shall check his findings with mine, on the barometer I have brought with me. [*sighs contentedly*] That should cover all the most important scientific aspects.

TATIANA: So why did you want the rest of us here?

NIKOLAI [*gently*]: All of us, Tatiana dear, can make some contribution to human knowledge, even if we are NOT astronomers. It is also important that the behaviour of animals and plants be observed at the moment of total eclipse, as well as our own personal impressions. So you TOO will have your chance. I trust you've brought your notebook.

TATIANA [*sighs in a bored fashion*]: Yeeeees!

NIKOLAI: Good. [*He begins unpacking his equipment*] But where are all the others? The er – you know. [*snaps his fingers*] Oh I'm not good at names – the butterfly catchers.

VARENKA [*with sweet malice*]: They got tired of waiting for you, as we all did, and went home to play cwoquet.

NIKOLAI: Croquet? Croquet!!! On this historic day? Ha! It's thanks to the indolence of our effete aristocracy that Russia is going to the dogs.

KOOZMA: There's till plenty of us here though, Nikolai. I'll go and round up the others.

IRINA [*in a peremptory tone*]: You DID remember to bring out the picnic blankets, I trust, Tatiana?

TATIANA [*coolly*]: Yes, Irina-Ivanevna, I DID remember to bring them!

IRINA: Good! Well, [*She smiles around*] I'd better see the General gets some coffee.

IRINA *and* KOOZMA *exeunt*

NIKOLAI [*calls after them*]: Make haste! [*He continues unpacking his bag, muttering the name of each item as he unearths it.*] ... barometer ... smoked glass. Have you got some smoked glass, Varenka.

VARENKA *ostentatiously ignores him*

NIKOLAI: I've brought some for you in case you forgot. [*shyly*] You mustn't damage those eyes.

VARENKA *pouts, but her expression softens*

TATIANA [*watches them enviously, folds her arms*]: How much longer! [*after a long pause, to herself, almost through tears*] Oh I do get so tired of carrying things around for people and just waiting for something to happen.

NIKOLAI: Where's the blanket?

TATIANA *hands it to him and it is laid on the grass*

NIKOLAI [*draws out his watch*]: My goodness just look at the time.

VARENKA [*in a little girl's voice*]: What causes eclipses to happen, Nikolai?

NIKOLAI [*importantly clears his throat*]: An eclipse of the sun occurs when the moon, passing through the plane of the E-clip-tic, assumes a position upon the line joining the centres of the sun and the earth.

VARENKA: Weally? How intewesting! And what does E-E ... you know, mean?

TATIANA *sighs irritably*

NIKOLAI: Ecliptic? Well, the adjective means – constituting or pertaining to the sun's apparent path in the sky, OR, pertaining to an eclipse.

TATIANA, *noisily and gigantically yawns.* VARENKA *frowns at her*

NIKOLAI: And the noun means: The apparent path of the sun around the earth: the plane passing through the sun's centre which contains the orbit of the earth, OR, [*He describes a circle with his hands*] a great circle ...

Once again TATIANA *interrupts his flow with a very noisy yawn. Both* VARENKA *and* NIKOLAI *cast a disapproving glance at her*

VARENKA: Pway go on, Nicolas.

NIKOLAI: OR, a great circle on the terrestrial globe, answering to, AND falling within, the plane of the celestial e-clip-tic.

VARENKA [*thinks hard for a long moment*]: And when you look through smoked glass, can you see the line joining the centre of the sun and earth?

NIKOLAI [*pauses*]: Varenka, my dear, the line is imaginary.

VARENKA [*completely bewildered*]: But if the line is imaginary, how can the moon assume a position on it?

NIKOLAI *amazed at the naïvety of such a question, tries to control his temper*

NIKOLAI: It's perfectly simple ...

TATIANA [*interrupts*]: Ha, Astronomy – I think it's all rubbish. How can anyone possibly foretell the future.

NIKOLAI [*icily*]: THAT is Astrology.

TATIANA [*sullenly*]: Anyway, YOU'VE never been up in the sky, Nikolai, so how can you tell what's going to happen to the sun and the moon. I bet you're just making it up.

VARENKA: Oh, Tania, don't be so twivial! You're such a cwoss-patch today. You must have got up out of the wong side of bed.

TATIANA: It's so long ago I can't remember. [*yawns*] Where's Koozma got to?

NIKOLAI: My God! Look at the time. We must prepare ourselves.

VARENKA: Here they come. [KOOZMA *and* IRINA *come onstage*] Where's Nastasia-Timofeyevna, and Anna-Ivanevna?

KOOZMA [*embarrassed*]: Well er, they, er – d-didn't want to get mud on their gowns.

VARENKA: How pedestwian!

TATIANA: Typical!

IRINA [*scolds*]: I did advise you last evening NOT to invite them, Koozma. I did suggest that . . .

KOOZMA [*interrupts*]: But Irina-Ivanevna, they d-d-didn't know it was going to rain, d-d-did they. But don't worry, Nikolai, they've b-brought their notebooks, and p-promised to observe the m-m-mammals through the window.

NIKOLAI [*coldly*]: And the Captain in the Hussars and his friend?

IRINA [*sourly*]: They WERE coming out, Nikolai, till the young ladies deliberately waylaid them. There'll be no prising them out now.

NIKOLAI: Huh! Characteristic of our degenerate aristocracy the so-called erudite class. And the General?

IRINA: Well he's – er, having a little refreshment. But he is seated by the barometer, Nikolai, dear, and he's promised to take notes.

NIKOLAI [*angrily draws out his watch*]: It's almost time. Kindly take your notebooks and smoked glass.

The others swoop on the table and equip themselves. KOOZMA *adopts an "artistic" pose, drawing distances by pressing the pencil to the end of his nose, and stretching his arm out full length*

TATIANA *stares straight ahead through her smoked glass. She lowers it*

TATIANA: Ooooooh!!! [*She scribbles something in her notebook*]

NIKOLAI: Now! ... I must note down our precise geographical position. [*He begins fiddling with his equipment*]

It begins to get darker

VARENKA: Oh look! Look everyone – a black spot's moving acwoss the sun. Oh, isn't it exciting.

NIKOLAI: Mesdames, Monsieur. Speed is of the essence. Please make your observations.

It becomes very silent as everyone looks up. KOOZMA *begins sketching.* TATIANA *begins to giggle, then her laughter becomes hysterical*

TATIANA: I'm f-frightened ... I don't like it – I feel funny. I don't like it. [*She grabs* KOOZMA*'s arm*]

NIKOLAI: I must remember to note the time to the exact second.

IRINA: Oh d-dear me. It's uncanny ... I don't think I feel safe. [*She grabs* KOOZMA*'s other arm*]

KOOZMA *stands, as if crucified, with the sketchbook in one hand and his pencil in the other, trying to struggle free*

IRINA [*whimpers*]: I've got a terrible headache.

TATIANA [*wails*]: I feel sick.

NIKOLAI [*shouts*]: What are you standing like that for, Koozma? DAMNIT MAN, sketch the Corona.

KOOZMA *indicates his helplessness by trying to shrug, but the two women have him firmly pegged. The two women continue whimpering*

NIKOLAI: I must measure the diameter.

VARENKA, *who hitherto has been staring up through her smoked glass, becomes infected by the panic of the other two women*

VARENKA: Oh d-d-dear – isn't it getting dark.

TATIANA [*hysterically*]: I think the world's coming to an end.

IRINA: What will become of us all? [*She crosses herself*]

VARENKA [*grabs* NIKOLAI*'s arm*]: Oh Nikolai – I'm fwightened. But it's made me wealise what's weally important to me. Let's meet in the summerhouse after.

NIKOLAI [*shakes her off*]: Don't hamper me, woman! Every second counts.

VARENKA: But I'm tewwified! [*She grabs* NIKOLAI *again, and he drops his smoked glass, and as he bends to retrieve it his sunglasses fall off*]

NIKOLAI: Look what you've done. Now I've dropped my glasses.

VARENKA *grabs him again and they fall in a heap. The women squeal as the sky becomes completely black. Slowly it begins to lighten, and* NIKOLAI *grovels about trying to locate his pencil and notebook*

NIKOLAI: Ah, there's my smoked glass. [*He straightens up and gazes skywards*] It's over ... [*His shoulders slump*] It's ... OVER!!!

TATIANA: Well thank goodness for that.

NIKOLAI [*brokenly*]: It's over ...

VARENKA: Oh good! [*tenderly*] Look at me, Nikolai.

NIKOLAI: It's OVER!!! [*He hisses*] The eclipse has come and gone, and I missed it.

VARENKA: Never mind dear. Now we can go to the summer-house.

NIKOLAI [*hollow voiced*]: It's over ... all my preparations come to nothing.

KOOZMA [*snaps at* TATIANA]: If you hadn't g-grabbed my arm, I could have sketched the c-c-corona.

TATIANA: Well don't go blaming me. [*Turns to* NIKOLAI] At least I did what you asked me to Nikolai. Honestly! Just before the eclipse, I saw a grey dog chasing a ginger cat. Then it wagged its tail for EVER such a long time. Look – I wrote it down.

NIKOLAI: Oh, this is the absolute limit. Now I am really provoked. [*He looks at his equipment, spreads wide his hands*] All my preparations to no avail!

IRINA [*who has been examining a flower bed, looks up to the sky*] [*vaguely*]: It's beginning to spit with rain again. Come along everyone, let's go into the warm and have some coffee.

She begins to walk off, followed by the others

TATIANA: Aren't you coming too, Nikolai.

NIKOLAI: If I did I wouldn't be responsible for my actions. I am a vi-o-lent man, when my plans are thwarted.

IRINA, *oblivious of the tension, walks on*

VARENKA: Oh but Nicolas – please, do come.

NIKOLAI: I shall never set foot in this place again, not so long as I live or breathe. Adieu!!! [*With as much dignity as he can muster in his goloshes, he begins to walk in the other direction*]

VARENKA [*races after him and wails*]: Oh Nicolas! [*She bursts into tears and races off past her mother*]

IRINA [*hurries back to* NIKOLAI]: Try not to take any notice, Nicolas! Give her time, dear, give her time. After all you've only known each other two short weeks. Ah! Such a loving nature she has, such a loving nature. [*confidentially*] Her Grandfather was Armenian you know. [*She taps his cheek consolingly*] Try not to despair, dear. She will come round in time – just leave her alone for the moment. [IRINA *begins hurrying away, then pauses*] Courage, mon brave, bon courage! [*She blows him a kiss*]

She exits leaving NIKOLAI *alone on stage*

NIKOLAI: Oh this is TOO much! This is really too much. Are they all mad?? It's not love seething in my breast, it's hatred. And if it weren't for fear of offending against social decorum, I should damned well tell Mashenka so ... Ah, but how can you tell a woman you don't love her, how can one?? ... It's as tactless as telling a writer he can't write ... [*He shivers, turns up his collar and looks at the sky*] And it'll be too blasted cold to sit out on my balcony and write. [*He angrily kicks at a pencil, and notebook on the ground, then disconsolately trudges offstage leaving his equipment behind*]

Lights slowly dim to complete blackout

End of Scene Five

Scene Six

A Russian choir in the distance is singing "EVENING BELLS" (Becherni Zbon). Lights come up very slowly. THE GENERAL *is seated alone in* IRINA*'s garden listening to the music*

GENERAL: Beautiful evening . . . [*listens to the choir*] . . . beautiful –
Listen to that . . . [*breathes deeply on the scented air*] Ah Russia
– Mother Russia. [*He recites a four line poem on nature – The
music swells – He looks up at the sky*] . . . A black grouse . . .
don't often see one of them these days . . . I remember
when it was teeming around here with woodcock, geese
and curlew . . . What are they doing to you, Mother Russia,
eh? Felling the forests, Pah!

KOOZMA *enters*

KOOZMA: Sir? . . . Beg your pardon, Sir. I d-didn't catch what you
said.

GENERAL: Oh . . . just thinkin' out loud, Koozma. Good evenin'
me boy.

KOOZMA: Good evening, Sir. B-b-beautiful evening.

GENERAL: Yes . . . enjoy it while you may . . . yes, I remember when
the country around here was alive with woodcock and
snipe – teal even! . . . They're all dyin' out – it's felling the
forests is causing it – deforestation, damnit! They chop
down the trees and the earth dries out – then the bracken
becomes combustible – only takes a few hot days, or a spark
from a pipe for the whole blasted lot to ignite – goes up like
tinder. [*sighs*] Some of the birds escape of course, but with
all the insects destroyed, what's there left for them to feed
on – eh? That's why they're dyin' out . . . As for the animals
– hardly ever see a wolf these days – as for a bear . . .

KOOZMA [*lights a small cigar*]: That's what m-m-my Uncle says.

GENERAL: The ponds and the lakes are all drying up – can't catch
a decent sized pike these days – time was when you could
catch a pike two feet long – [*He stretches out his arms*] – two
feet long . . . there used to be turbot, bream . . . And when

d'you see a swarm of wild honey bees these days . . . What's it gonna be like a hundred years from now, eh?

KOOZMA: You do sound in a g-g-gloomy mood, Sir.

GENERAL: Well . . . just glad I won't be around to see it [*sighs*] Yes, everything has its compensations – even old age. [*He suddenly chuckles*] But speaking of gloom – here comes our Hamlet.

NIKOLAI *enters, picks up a pencil from the grass, and looks around for his other equipment.* THE GENERAL *continues quietly chuckling*

GENERAL: I gather his eclipse didn't go according to plan. [*chortles*] Sorry I missed it.

KOOZMA *joins in with his laughter*

GENERAL [*calls out*]: Good evenin' Nikolai me boy. Come and join us.

NIKOLAI *reluctantly crosses to join them*

GENERAL: Varenka WILL be pleased to see you. She's been goin' round all day with a face as long as a pike staff.

NIKOLAI [*firmly*]: I haven't come to visit, Vladimir Sergeyevitch, merely to collect my equipment.

KOOZMA: They took it up to the house yesterday afternoon, N-N-Nikolai – because of the rain.

GENERAL [*to* NIKOLAI]: Haven't seen you around today. [*innocently*] Been working on your thesis on the eclipse have you, me boy?

NIKOLAI*'s lips tighten. He casts a suspicious glance at* THE GENERAL, *but makes no reply*

GENERAL: Yes . . . I did as you asked me yesterday by the way, – measured the temperature on the barometer for you – gave me notes to Irina-Ivanevna.

NIKOLAI [*icily*]: I'd rather not discuss it if you don't mind.

KOOZMA: Would you c-c-care for a cigarette, Nicolai?

NIKOLAI *accepts the cigarette and light*

NIKOLAI [*distantly*]: Thank you.

GENERAL: Oh, and by the by – I made a few enquiries round, among me servants and friends. It appears quite a number of extraordinary occurrences took place during the time of the eclipse – quite extraordinary, Yes! Sheer pandemonium!!!

NIKOLAI – *hooked, gets out his notebook*

GENERAL: If you'd care to make a few notes. Well, according to my herdsman, cows, horses and sheep bolted all over the fields, bellowing in terror, with their tails straight up in the air.

KOOZMA [*seriously*]: Even the sh-sh-sheep's tails, Sir?

GENERAL [*gravely*]: Even the sheep's tails, Koozma.

NIKOLAI *takes notes*

GENERAL: And apparently a local Sexton who was bringing a load of cucumbers home from his allotment panicked – jumped off his cart, and hid under the bridge. And the horse pulling his cart bolted into someone's yard, where the cucumbers were all devoured by the pigs. And! [*confidentially*] This is a bit spicy, Koozma. [*chuckles*] An Excise Officer, who had been staying the night at a "certain" lady's dacha, [*He smooths back his moustache*] ran out among the crowd, wearing just his underwear, shouting wildly: "Every man for himself."

KOOZMA [*chuckles*]: I s-s-say, you're having us on aren't you, Sir?

GENERAL: NO! And listen to this. Many of the youngest and prettiest guests in the dachas, were woken by the noise and dashed out with no shoes on. [*lowers his voice*] And all sorts of other things occurred, Koozma me lad, which I hesitate to recount.

KOOZMA *begins chuckling and becomes helpless with laughter. He winces, grabs hold of his hip, straightens his leg, and both he and* THE GENERAL *continue roaring with laughter*

NIKOLAI *snaps his notebook shut*

NIKOLAI: I am afraid I see no humour whatsoever in the situation. [*He stalks off leaving both* THE GENERAL *and* KOOZMA *still helpless with mirth*]

GENERAL [*calming down a little*]: Poor Nikolai takes everything so seriously. [*He begins chuckling again*] Here ... what about this?

KOOZMA *mops his eyes and listens*

GENERAL: Strangest thing of all! Bedbugs – thinking it was night again, crept out of their nooks and crannies, and began biting anyone who was still asleep. [*He slaps his thigh and continues laughing*]

KOOZMA *is helpless with mirth*

KOOZMA: I don't think we're meeting with Nikolai's approval. [*They continue chuckling*]

GENERAL: He's too set in his ways – old-maidish! He could do a lot worse than marry Varenka – shake him up a bit. [*confidentially*] Her Grandfather was Armenian you know. Spent some time in Armenia in me young days – very hot-blooded race the Armenians. I should know – I was Military Attache at Erevan for three years. [*He almost drools at the memory*] [*sighs*] Oh yes! I could tell you a thing or two. Did you know that ... [*He whispers something in* KOOZMA*'s ear*]

KOOZMA: NO!!! [*splutters with laughter*] D-d-d-do they???

GENERAL [*to* KOOZMA]: Oh yes, and ... [*whispers again*]

TATIANA *comes into the garden and calls out*

TATIANA: Good evening, Nikolai.

further laughter from the two men. TATIANA *crosses to join them*

TATIANA: What are you two laughing about?

KOOZMA: Nothing that would be suitable for your d-d-delicate ears.

TATIANA [*tartly*]: Ah well – in that case save it for Nastasia-Timofeyevna and Anna-Ivanevna. Anyway, I can't stay. Irina would like to know if you're ready for an aperitif?

GENERAL: Ready, aye, ready. Always ready!

KOOZMA: Just the thing.

TATIANA *crosses towards* NIKOLAI. *As the two men start to leave,* THE GENERAL *calls over his shoulder*

GENERAL: Are you coming in for a drink, Nikolai?

NIKOLAI: Thank you – NO!!

The two men exit

TATIANA: I think it will be most unkind if you don't come into the house, Nikolai. Varenka's been moping all day.

NIKOLAI [*embarrassed*]: Well, I will perhaps just call in – to collect my equipment.

TATIANA: She hasn't stopped weeping.

NIKOLAI [*touched*]: Really?

TATIANA: Here she comes now – I'll go and pick some flowers.

VARENKA, *looking pale and wan, wanders on, pretending she is miles away.* NIKOLAI *goes up to her*

NIKOLAI [*shyly*]: Er, good evening, Varenka.

silence

NIKOLAI: I'm glad to see you, how are you?

VARENKA *bursts into tears, throws her arms around his neck*

VARENKA: Oh Nicolas! At last, at last! Where have you been? I didn't sleep all night. I've been pondewing and pondewing, and I feel if I DID get to know you better, I could – WOULD – come to love you.

NIKOLAI *manages to disentangle himself from her arms*

NIKOLAI: Well, erm – I'm afraid I do – erm, have certain rather definite views on marriage. [*He becomes interested in his lecture*] For example, there are certain aspects held by the Hindu sects, AND certain of the Egyptians, with their intriguing ideas on wedlock with which I am in complete agreement, and . . .

VARENKA [*interrupts*]: Oh Nicolas, DON'T twy my patience so badly.

NIKOLAI [*engrossed in his subject*]: And then, to come to more recent times, certain of Schopenhauer's ideas merit consideration. There is, to take as an instance, his view that . . .

VARENKA [*who has been watching him with adoring eyes, interrupts again*]: Oh, Nicolas – give me a kiss.

NIKOLAI [*surprised*]: What a curious non sequitur!

VARENKA: Nicolas – give me a kiss.

After a moment's pause, he kisses her cheek, primly, with some distaste, as though it were the cheek of his dead grandmother

TATIANA *and* IRINA *come into the garden arm in arm. When* IRINA *spies the couple, she unceremoniously tries to push* TATIANA *out of sight*

IRINA: Shhh! Go away girl – do something. Pick some flowers!

She is going to follow TATIANA, *then excitedly rushes over to the couple*

IRINA: Oh may God bless you both! Take good care of her, Nikolai. Come Varenka, we must tell the others. Oh, let's have champagne in the garden. [*She ushers* VARENKA *towards the house, then hurries back to* NIKOLAI] And Nikolai dear, NEVER forget the sacrifice she is making.

As she hurries away, the village choir in the distance can be heard singing a lively version of "BLACKEYES". NIKOLAI – *stunned, sinks onto the nearest chair with his mouth open*

As the lights slowly fade, the choir continues singing till the lights come up on the last scene

End of Scene Six

Scene Seven

NIKOLAI *is seated at the wooden table in* IRINA*'s garden, writing*

NIKOLAI: September 6th, 1887. [*He sighs and gazes into space. Begins writing*] Have made little progress with my thesis since my marriage. [*He blots what he has written*] Only another week in which to complete it, and then back to City life and Accountancy. [*He sighs and straightens up*] Still if I put my mind to it, it can be done. It CAN be done! [*He addresses the audience*] But every time my thoughts take wing, she presses up against me saying, "To think we are now wed, and you are mine – MINE! ... Tell me you love me, TELL me, darling" ... and those eyes - like black velvet. [*He shakes his head to clear his thoughts*] Enough! [*grumbles*] And Irina-Ivanevna with her eternal damned soirées, all those guests with their endless, mindless prattle – never a moment to myself. No, dammit, I will NOT put up with it! They will find out that it is better not to meddle with me. Lead a vi-o-lent man like me to the altar, and you had better watch out! I demand peace and quiet to continue my studies. [*mournfully*] Ah! Will posterity ever know what this thesis has cost me ... Get to work, Nikolai – get to work ... Devil's teeth, where have I put my notes? [*He picks up a sheet of notepaper scans through it and begins angrily writing*]

THE GENERAL *wanders into the garden. He prods the ground, muttering to himself*

GENERAL: Crabgrass! ... No, it's not looking the same as when the Krilov's had it. No, damnit – it's not ... Mind you the Krilovs didn't keep a table like Irina-Ivanevna, that they didn't ... Superb cook. Superb! Shouldn't think there'd be much chance of prising her away from Irina-Ivanevna – still, no harm in trying ... nothing venture, nothing gain. [*prods again*] Chickweed! [*He spies* NIKOLAI *and calls out*] Ah, good afternoon, Nikolai. So THAT'S where you've got to. Varenka and Irina-Ivanevna sent me out here to try to winkle you out – see what you were up to.

NIKOLAI *gives a brief stiff smile, and returns to his notes*

THE GENERAL *looks up at the sky*

GENERAL [*mutters*]: Days are getting shorter ... misty evenings ...
[*the sound of a curlew calling*] Curlews crying ... cranes are
flying ... Huntin' will start soon. [THE GENERAL *sighs*] Ah
well – s'pose I'd better join the dour Nikolai – jolly him up.
[*takes a few paces*] But after last night's farewell do for the
Hussars, am I really up to "The Dog Tax, its Past and
Future"?? NO!! [*shakes his head decisively, clutches it and
winces. Walks on a few paces, glances back at* NIKOLAI] Always
looks so gloomy when Varenka's not around ... She's done
him the world of good – the world of good. [*He strolls on in
the direction of his estate.*]

KOOZMA [*comes into the garden and crosses to join* NIKOLAI. *He is in
excellent spirits*]: Hello there, Nikolai. Hard at it, I see. How's
the writing going? [*He seats himself next to* NIKOLAI.]

NIKOLAI: Oh ... very well – very well.

KOOZMA [*enthusiastically rubs his hands together*]: Yes, so's mine,
so's mine! M-managed to complete a whole chapter yesterday afternoon.

NIKOLAI [*surprised and envious*]: A whole chapter??? I suppose
that was ... after ... Tatiana ... [*Not knowing how to complete
the sentence, he leaves it unsaid.*]

KOOZMA: Yes – erm ... after T-Tatiana ...

NIKOLAI *returns to his notes*

KOOZMA: I see the General's taking the air.

pause

NIKOLAI [*trying to concentrate*]: Yeeeees.

KOOZMA: Marvellous for his age, don't you th-think?

long pause

NIKOLAI: Yes, marvellous.

KOOZMA: Still got an eye for the ladies, though.

pause

KOOZMA: When he's not thinking about his s-s-stomach. [*chuckles to himself*] But I think his stomach takes first place – eh what, Nikolai? [*Getting no response, he raises his voice*] I said I think his stomach takes first place, what say you, Nikolai?

NIKOLAI [*grits his teeth*]: YES!

KOOZMA [*stretches out his legs*]: This is the sort of weather I like – sunny, cool breeze, not too h-h-hot.

long silence

KOOZMA: Mind you I think we deserved it after all that rain ... Plays the very d-d-devil with that wound in my hip ... seemed as if the rain would never end – went on right through August ... They haven't got the oats in yet I've heard ... Bad for the peasants – not much help for the owners either – certainly not their b-b-bank balances ... [*sighs*] [*smiles*] Yes, but you b-b-being an accountant will know all about that.

NIKOLAI *screws up a piece of paper and throws it to the ground*

KOOZMA: I say, I'm not interfering with your c-c-concentration, am I.

NIKOLAI [*icily*]: NOT – AT – ALL!

THE GENERAL [*joins them*]: Good afternoon, Koozma-Maximovitch. I say, you're cutting a splendid figure – done up like a dog's dinner. [*He seats himself*] I hear you were all up at the Sumowski's last evening – enjoy yourselves?

KOOZMA: Yes splendid, s-splendid, wasn't it Nikolai?

NIKOLAI [*after a long pause*]: Yes, splendid.

GENERAL: Heard there were a lot of pretty girls present. I couldn't attend myself, unfortunately – had other commitments ... Yes, sorry I missed that ... I hear Tatiana-Maximovna left for Novgorod this morning?

KOOZMA: Yes, yes ... Ch-charming girl. We all saw her off on the t-train didn't we, Nikolai?

NIKOLAI [*looks up vaguely*]: What ... oh, yes.

GENERAL: SHE left in the deuce of a hurry, didn't she.

KOOZMA [*with a suppressed grin*]: Yes – er, I suppose one could say that – erm, family affairs, I understand ... s-s-something like that.

GENERAL: Erm. [*curiously*] Tell me, Koozma ...

KOOZMA: Sir??

GENERAL: Er, no matter, no matter ... And you Nikolai-Andreyevitch. When do you and the family decamp for Petersburgh? Irina-Ivanevna did tell me, but it must've slipped me mind.

NIKOLAI: We have just another week here, Vladimir-Sergeyevitch. September the 12th to be pre-cise.

GENERAL: Ah yes! So soon? What about you, Koozma lad?

KOOZMA: Oh, I'm in no rush, S-Sir, now the weather's changed. Anyway – er, q-quite a lot of p-pleasant happenings still seem to be t-taking place here, and in any case I intend now really putting in some work on my Memoirs. Once the S-Social season starts in M-Moscow, there'll be p-precious little time. Better to do it here in the peace and tranquillity of the c-countryside, eh what, Nikolai?

NIKOLAI [*scowls*]: Huh!

GENERAL: Er – tell me, Koozma ...

KOOZMA: Sir???

GENERAL: No matter, no matter ... The Hussars have completed their summer manoeuvres you know ... [*sadly*] I shall miss the lads.

KOOZMA: Yeees, Anna-Ivanevna did m-m-mention the Hussars were moving on ... Yeees, [*trying to hide his delighted grin*] Yeees, sh-sh-shame about that.

GENERAL: That should quieten things down a bit, now they've moved on. Some of the Officers came up last night, for a farewell drink. [*He sniffs the air*] Then the autumn – me favourite season, get in a bit of shooting – bag a few pheasant. Beats women any day – [*chuckles drily*] At least at my time of life it does. [*pause*] Tell me, Koozma ...

KOOZMA: Sir???

GENERAL: Oh nothing important. How's the thesis comin' along, Nikolai?

NIKOLAI [*sarcastically*]: Oh I manage to get a little done very occasionally when there are no interruptions.

KOOZMA [*draws out his watch*]: Good Lord! Well I'll bid you good afternoon, gentlemen.

GENERAL: Where are you rushin' off to?

KOOZMA [*dreamy smile*]: Oh, I've been invited to take t-t-tea with N-Nastasia-Timofeyevna, and Anna-Ivanevna. Time's getting on. I'd better be on my way. [*He bows to each of the men and begins to leave*]

GENERAL [*calls after him*]: Tell me, Koozma ...

KOOZMA [*reluctantly halts*]: Sir???

GENERAL: No matter, no matter ... [*then decisively*] No dammit, why shouldn't I ask! Tell me Koozma how DID you manage to escape the clutches of the Titanic Tatiana? I thought your head was well and truly in the noose there.

KOOZMA [*trying not to look too pleased with himself*]: Well, you see ... [*He takes a few paces in their direction*] Well, it so happens – I h-h-have this old friend from my f-former regiment – a medico – useful actually, and h-h-he was able to s-supply me with a medical certificate, which p-p-proves that *as* a result of that w-wound in my temple I am – so to speak, non compos mentis, and therefore – legally debarred from getting married. [*He controls his smile*] So, after all, it wouldn't have been f-f-fair on the girl, would it? – Not the g-g-gentlemanly thing to do. Now, if you will excuse me, I must take leave of your dear wife, and Mother-in-law, Nikolai. [*He bows to each of them*] Good afternoon, Gentlemen. [*He exits*]

After some seconds silence, during which time NIKOLAI *has sat stony-faced,* THE GENERAL *begins quietly chuckling.* NIKOLAI *glances irritably at him, then once again begins writing.* THE GENERAL *chuckles again. His laughter grows louder*

GENERAL: Brilliant! Brilliant! You see, as I've always maintained, Nikolai – everything has its positive side – even a bullet wound in the head. You should've taken a leaf from his book my boy. [*sighs*] Well, give a man credit, where credit's due. Koozma's not quite so stupid as he'd have us all believe.

NIKOLAI *scowls, and continues furiously scribbling.* THE GENERAL *draws out his watch*

GENERAL: Irina-Ivanevna promised me tea and pastries. Better see what's happenin' on the kitchen front. Sorry I can't keep you company lad. But, why not come with me?

NIKOLAI [*icily*]: No thank you, I have WORK to do.

THE GENERAL *hobbles offstage, and* NIKOLAI *moodily gazes into space*

NIKOLAI [*addresses audience*]: Yes it was brilliant – brilliant, dammit – BRILLIANT!!! A devilish cunning ruse – non compos mentis!! Why didn't I think of something like that? I could have got medical certificates too, proving mental instability in my own family. One of my uncles drank like a fish, and another was absent-minded to the point of imbecility. Did he not once, when leaving an important Court gala, put a lady's fur muff on his head, instead of his fur hat? . . . And what of my Aunt Galina? She used to poke out her tongue at men in the street – yes! AND, wasn't she always playing the grand piano??? And then there's PAUVRE Maman! Did she not ACTUALLY SAY, on hearing the news of my coming marriage – "At last! At last! My dream has come true". [*smiles tragically*] If that be not proof of a sadly unhinged mind, then I know not what is? [*He continues as though he is addressing a jury*] And then, ladies and Gentlemen. Take the evidence of my own extreme quick-temperedness – a very dubious symptom. To cross my path, as is well known, is as risky a business as putting one's hand in a frenzied tiger's cage . . . [*sighs*] Non compos mentis – what a good idea! Why do good ideas always come too late?

VARENKA [*voice off*]: Nikolai darling – what are you doing?

NIKOLAI [*hisses*]: SHE had better watch out. [*sweetly*] I'm working on my thesis.

VARENKA [*enters, and smiles at him indulgently*]: Well put that silly thing away, pwecious. We have to get weady.

NIKOLAI: Ready for what?

VARENKA: Scatterbwain. Have you forgotten? We're dining with Count Kuznitski, and you know how long it takes you to dwess, and I want you to look especially nice. My beautiful new husband. [*She presses his head to her bosom, and covers it with kisses*] My litewawy lion. Now huwwy up! [*She exits singing*]

NIKOLAI: She had better beware of my choleric rages.

VARENKA [*voice off, irritably*]: Huwwy up! Put that silly thing away! You don't want me to get cwoss again, now do you?

NIKOLAI: Non compos mentis. Why do good ideas always come too late? [*decisively*] I shall NOT go. I have important work to do. I shall refuse, damnit!

VARENKA *pokes her head round the corner*

VARENKA [*languorously*]: Come along pwecious. I want you to help me get dwessed. And you know what a butterfingers I am with fastenings.

NIKOLAI [*sighs tremulously*]: Coming darling . . . coming.

FINAL CURTAIN

To rousing chorus of the peasants singing "BLACK-EYES"

"THE DENTAL SURGEON"

by

Anton Chekov

(Translated and freely adapted by Elizabeth Gamberoni)

ХИРУРГИЯ

(Only the lowly orders in the Russian Orthodox Church wore plaits. The higher orders wore their hair very much like Rasputin – and still do.)

Characters in order of appearance

STEPAN-STEPANICH KOORYATIN. (A middle-aged Medical Orderly)

MASHA. (A middle-aged Housekeeper)

VONMEEGLAZOV. (An elderly Sexton)

SOPHIA (Masha's daughter), voice off

The action takes place in a small village hospital, some miles from the nearest town. The surgery is almost bare, apart from a large wooden table on which rests an appointment book, an inkwell, and a quill, and, at the very edge of the table a large bottle labelled "carbolic acid".

Upstage to the left is a rustic armchair, and next to it a small table with a dish that contains surgical instruments. Next to this is a small stool, and lying on the floor close by, a small heap of blood-stained dressings

MUSIC – a lively Russian folkdance.

The stage is empty until the medical orderly KOORYATIN *enters. He is fortyish, thickset, and is wearing threadbare trousers, no socks, and down at heel shoes. Over his shirt is an ancient, none too clean white jacket, which is too small for him, and has split at the elbows.*

The music gradually fades.

KOORYATIN *surveys himself with some pleasure in the mirror to the far right of the stage. He pulls down the white jacket over his paunch, smooths back his hair, then smiles at his reflection in the mirror. He draws deeply on his cheap cigar struts downstage a few paces, and blows out a stream of smoke in a grandiose manner. He surveys his surroundings with some content, then seats himself at the table, draws the appointment book towards him and studies it.*

MASHA *the housekeeper enters. She is plump, middle-aged, and wears an apron over her long black dress. She is carrying a feather duster, as well as a dustpan and brush. Sighting* KOORYATIN, *she flaps a hand in front of her face and gives vent to an histrionic cough.*

KOORYATIN *feigns not to have noticed*

MASHA [*coughs again. She speaks with a strong country dialect*]: What's that so-called cigar made of then, cowdung? Anyway you ain't got no right to be smokin' in yere.

KOORYATIN [*speaks with the same dialect*]: That be aint none of yore business. T'aint for the loikes of a common 'ouse-keeper like you, one who can't even read her letters, to be tellin' someone of the loikes of ME what to do.

MASHA [*sarcastically*: Oooh, jest look at 'im. Stepan Steepanich Kooryatin, the FAMOUS medical orderly. [*She flicks angrily around the rustic chair with her feather duster*] Done up loike a peacock 'e is since the Doctor's departure.

KOORYATIN *bestows a withering glance on her, pulls down his jacket, draws the inkwell towards him, dips in the quill, and makes a solitary tick in the book. He replaces the quill, puts his feet up on the table, leans back in his chair and blows a smoke ring at the ceiling*

MASHA *frowns, and sweeps the blood-stained dressings into her dustpan. Then she coughs again and flaps a hand in front of her face*

MASHA: Even Doctor Vissotski 'isself don't smoke in his surgery. 'E smokes in 'is study.

KOORYATIN: Well we aint all made in the same mould, is we? We acts the way we feels.

MASHA *channels her anger into dusting the stool, and then the medical instruments which rattle*

MASHA: If Doctor Vissotski could see you now, with yore great clod 'opping feet on his table, and . . .

KOORYATIN [*interrupts*]: Well he can't can 'e. And even if he could I don't s'pose it'd worry 'im. I 'spect he's got other things on his mind on 'is honeymoon, than worryin' 'bout me smoking in his surgery. [*He laughs uproariously and coarsely*] Oi bet 'e has!

MASHA *continues dusting with even more vigour*

KOORYATIN [*thinks of another joke and splutters with mirth*]: Oi bet, [*He explodes into laughter*] Oi bet he's thinking 'bout better parts of the 'uman anatomy than my feet. [*He chokes with amusement and mops his eyes*]

MASHA [*continues dusting, barely restricting the impulse to dust* KOOR-YATIN]: You ought to wash yore mouth out with some of that carbolic acid. [*short pause*] Huh!! Tellin' that stranger the other day that you was a Dental Surgeon. Huh! Even Doctor Vissotski isself don't brag about that.

KOORYATIN: He pulls teef don't 'e? Jest like any other doctor, don't 'e?

MASHA: Well of course he does. Every doctor does that.

KOORYATIN: Well then! [*He takes the quill and begins laboriously writing in the date*] Sunday the 17th day of . . .

MASHA *angrily dusts the table again, causing the instruments to rattle*

KOORYATIN: What you fartin' about doin' now?

MASHA: I'm cleaning the medical instruments. THAT'S what oi be doing. Loike I always does.

KOORYATIN: You spent 5 minutes buggerin' about doin' that yesterday.

MASHA: *And* I'll be spending five minutes doin' the same thing termorrow! Doctor Vissotski loikes things kept – [*She draws herself up to her full height before pronouncing the word*] I-gen-ic, he does.

KOORYATIN *ignores her and continues writing in the appointments book*

KOORYATIN: ... the 17th day of August, in the year of our Lord, 1884, which 'appens to be my birthday. [*He draws on his cigar*]

From outside can be heard the jingle of a bridle, some shouts and commotion

YOUNG GIRL [*voice off*]: Oh Mama, Mama come quickly, the Gipsy Pedlar's here. Come and see what he's brung. There's ribbons, and satins and and lots of things.

MASHA *stands indecisively for a moment, torn between spying on* KOORYATIN *and rushing outside*

YOUNG GIRL: Oh Mama, hurry. He's got spices and herbs, and pots and pans, and ribbons for my hair. Come quickly. He's got brooches and rings ... Come quickly!

MASHA [*calls out of the window*]: I'm coming, Sophia, I'm coming. [*She gathers together her shovel and brush and begins to leave. She pauses at the door to direct a last magnificent – HA!! - at Kooryatin before hurrying off*]

KOORYATIN: Nosey old sow' [*He reads out*] August 18th – cow expected to calve on the Krilov estate. That should be interestin' ... Well, nothin' much doin' here. Might as well celebrate me name day with a quick nip of vodka.

He checks his reflection in the mirror and exits to the study

After some seconds someone begins tapping on the outside door. The tapping is repeated. SEXTON VONMEEGLAZOV *pokes his head round the door. His head is covered with a gaily floral-sprigged black kerchief, tied on the top of his head with the two points sticking up, which gives him the appearance of a rabbit. This is to protect the abscess on his tooth. His large ears protrude from either side of the kerchief. He is elderly, and extremely tall and thin, and one of his eyes is almost closed with the pain from his tooth. He sidles his body round the door. He is clad in a brown cassock which reaches to his ankles, with a broad leather belt at the waist, and long felt boots. He stands irresolutely at the door, then examines the room*

VONMEEGLAZOV [*groans*]: Oooo [*in a singsong manner, as in church*] O Lord ... Kind Saint Nicholas ... Holy Mother of God [*to himself*] Don't seem to be an ikon anywhere hereabouts. Funny that! [*He distractedly crosses himself in front of the bottle of carbolic acid. To attract attention he gives voice to a painful cough. As nobody comes, he coughs again, then cautiously knocks on the table. After a long silence he wails out loud, gazes round the room. Knocks more decisively on the table, and coughs again very loudly*]

KOORYATIN *hurries in, wiping his mouth with the back of his hand. He straightens up when he sees he has a patient, crosses to him with a certain deference*

KOORYATIN: Ah yes – Um, your excell ... Oh it's you Sexton. To what do we own this honner? [*He points to the chair*] Pray be seated!

THE SEXTON *inclines his head, then hands* KOORYATIN *a small bundle wrapped up in cloth*

KOORYATIN: Oh yes ... er, what is it?

VONMEEGLAZOV: Communion bread – left over from the service. Already blessed it be ... I spect you'd like some.

KOORYATIN [*Not impressed*]: Much obliged I'm sure. [*He deposits it on the table, businesslike*] Well, sit yourself down.

THE SEXTON *sits down and* KOORYATIN *drags up the stool next to him.* VONMEEGLAZOV *tenderly touches his jaw. He casts tortured eyes to Heaven and groans*

KOORYATIN: Now' What brings you 'here? ... What's ailing you?

THE SEXTON *doesn't immediately reply. He again glances heavenwards and groans, then remembering the courtesies, stands up and drops a deep bow*

VONMEEGLAZOV: Excuse me I was forgetting. The blessing of this Sabbath day be with you, Sergei Koozmich. Honour to your graceful person.

KOORYATIN [*jumps up and bows*]: Thank you, and the same to you. Now let's be gettin' on with it. Tell me, what's wrong with you?

VONMEEGLAZOV [*sighs*]: Ah! Verily and truly do it say in the psalms. [*He chants*] And thou shalt drink from my-y-y-y teeears. [*He holds the last note for some time, then abruptly seats himself*]

[*Pause*]

KOORYATIN: SO? Get on with it.

VONMEEGLAZOV [*In a mournful confidential manner*]: Well, I'll begin at the beginning. The other day it started, it was early in the morning, and I'd just sat down with the old woman to break our fast when thump, and as God is my witness I'd not even drunk one drop of tea – not so much as a dewdrop, nor one crumb of bread had passed my lips, when THUMP, and all my strength fled from me, and I wanted to lay me down to die, not the smallest crumb of bread, Sergei Koozmich, and all my strength seemed to have drained out of me into this very tooth. [*He opens his mouth and points*] If you would be so kind as to turn your benevolent attention onto it.

KOORYATIN: Well, if you get that thing off I'll have a look.

VONMEEGLAZOV *carefully unties the kerchief, flinching as he does so*

KOORYATIN, *through the smoke of his cigar peers into* VONMEEGLAZOV *'s mouth*

VONMEEGLAZOV *coughs and splutters, spitting onto* KOORYATIN *'s jacket. He brushes him down*

VONMEEGLAZOV: Ooh – sorry about that. Well, it's all down this one side, it thumps and it throbs, it resounds in me ears, it's just like a spike being hammered in, OR to take as another example, it's as if something's being shot through it. Yes! A shooting pain ... Tis a punishment for my wayful life. [*He chants*] And this is the price thou shalt pay for thy in-do-o-lence. [*He holds the last note, then sighs dejectedly*] Yes, it's for my sins, Sergei Koozmich, for me sins. After Liturgy the other day the Priest Eefray rebuked me, "A fat lot of good you are leading the singing," he said. "You open your mouth and one cannot make out a single word you're supposed to be singing. What sort of singing do you call it," he said, "when you don't even open your mouth?" [*sighs*] Well, Sergei Koozmich, judge for yourself – what sort of singing CAN one do, when you can't open your mouth cause of a swollen gum? AND – if you'll excuse my mentioning it, to make matters worse, not a wink of sleep I've had these past ...

His voice fades away as KOORYATIN *slowly gets up and approaches him. With the grave air of a connoisseur, he touches* THE SEXTON*'s cheekbones and pronounces*

KOORYATIN: Mmmmmmyes!

VONMEEGLAZOV: Mmmmmmyes???

KOORYATIN: Mmmyes. [*He stands up decisively and carries the stool to the table. He points dramatically*] Sit 'ere where I can get a better look at it.

THE SEXTON *sits on the stool, and looks up at* KOORYATIN *with terrified eyes*

KOORYATIN: Well – open your mouth!

THE SEXTON *opens it a fraction, eyeing* KOORYATIN *warily*

KOORYATIN: Wider! [*He takes* THE SEXTON*'s head in both hands, bends it right back and looks inside the mouth. He turns the head to the right and gazes in, then turns it to the left and has a further look. He licks his index finger, wipes it on his jacket, then pokes it into* THE SEXTON*'s mouth. As it lands on the abscessed tooth,* THE SEXTON *lets out a howl*] [*sagely*] I reckon THAT must be the one.

THE SEXTON *groans*

KOORYATIN: All right all right all right – keep yore hair on. No need to make all that fuss. Jest sit quiet for a minute while I work out the best way to deal with it.

VONMEEGLAZOV: I tried all manner of things – aniseed, cloves . . . The Deacon's father told me to soak horseradish in vodka and apply that to it. [*He sighs and adds bleakly*] It didn't help. Then Madame Gleekeria Anneeseemova – may the good Lord preserve her, [*He crosses himself*] saintly lady that she is, told me to gargle with warm milk and keep it in me mouth, and she also give me a piece of thread what come from the Holy Mount Fonski to tie round me little finger. Well, the milk weren't no good – I couldn't maintain it, could I? What with it being Lent and the fast, and fearing God's punishment and all that. But it DID seem to me that the bit of thread from Mount Afonski WAS helping, and . . .

KOORYATIN [*interrupts*]: Superstitions! All superstitions. Old wive's tales! [*he peers again into the sexton's mouth*] It'll 'ave to come out.

VONMEEGLAZOV [*Timidly*]: Well I . . . I spose you knows best, Stepan–Stepanich. [*pause*] I mean that's what you're trained for, to understand these matters – whether to take a tooth out or not, or what drops to dole out to soothe it. What I always say is God bless benefactors and providers like yourself, healing the suffering of others like me. May the saints in heaven bless you, as day and night I'll bless yore shadow till you're carried to the grave, for knowing the right course of action to take.

KOORYATIN [*modestly*]: Oh it's nothink. Surgery's nothink once you know how. It's just a question of getting used to it, and firms hands. That's what you need – FIRM HANDS!! Then it's as easy as splittin' logs. [*He draws on his cigar and continues in an expansive manner*] Funny thing though – only the other day a gent come in here be the name of Alexander-Ivanovich Eegeepetski – got the same problem like you, a bad tooth. REAL gent he was, a big landowner, a heddicated man, asked me all manner of questions. Oh yes, we had a real old natter about this and that – jest the two of us, jest like it was you and me sitting here. [*He continues bragging*] A real toff! Lived in St. Petersburgh for six years he had, on nodding terms with all the professors. His suits cost him a hundred roubles apiece, a HUNDRED roubles! Sat here for a long time he did, and, like I told 'm "What you've got to understand Sir, is teeth is funny things. There's no two is alike," I said. "They've all got their funny little ways, you've jest got to understand them. Anyway, I give him an examination and said, "I'm afraid I'll have to yank it out yore Honner," AND, jest like you he said "Well you knows best, Sergei Koozmich." Called me be me first name he did – shook my hand. [*He draws on his cigar and smiles at the memory*] Oh yes! One of the Gentry! We 'ad a real good chinwag. [*He picks up the tray containing the surgical instruments*] Yeees – like I told Squire Alexander Ivanovich Eegeepetski. "Teef is funny things," I said. "You've got to treat each one in a different way. With some you need the pincers, with others it's better to kick off by making a traction with a knife, and then of course with the REAL obstinate buggers, it's better if you use the elevator. [*confidentially*] That's a sort of spanner. [*He demonstrates with his hands*] You just never can tell with teef. [*He picks up each implement separately and studies them, weighing the pros and cons. Finally. decisively, he seizes the pincers*]

While this is going on, THE SEXTON *watches his every move with wide frightened eyes. He crosses himself and gives a nervous cough*]

KOORYATIN *moves away from the table, and stands to the right of the audience facing* THE SEXTON

KOORYATIN: Right, Sir. Open your mouth wider. [*He peers into it*] Now – we'll, er ... erm ... won't take a jiffy. I'm only going to cut the gum. [*He takes a large penknife from his pocket, spits on both sides of the blade, and wipes it dry on his jacket*] Tractions have to be done on the vertical ... Here we go. [*He cuts and* THE SEXTON *shrieks*]

KOORYATIN [*gaily*]: Well! That wasn't no problem was it ... [*embarrassed*] Oh! ... Oh – Oh sorry about nicking your chin, but if you'd opened your mouth proper, I could've got to your gum instead.

VONMEEGLAZOV [*sourly*]: Thank you very much! Of course patients like me are only fools – benighted ones you might say, whereas you enlightened people …

KOORYATIN [*interrupts*]: Now you're being unreasonable. What d'you expect if you keep your gob shut. Let's have another go.

THE SEXTON *tenderly mops his chin with a grubby handkerchief*]

VONMEEGLAZOV: No! I've decided I don't want no traction. No … I'm not having that again.

KOORYATIN: Oh alright then, I'll do it without the traction, but don't start twitching like a rabbit. It's easy enough to yank them out once you get a good grip. One tug, and Sergei's your uncle. Jest you sit still and don't fidget.

VONMEEGLAZOV [*aggrievedly*]: How can I help fidgeting perched on this stool? I feel I'm going to fall off. I can't balance myself.

KOORYATIN: Well, sit on the chair if it'll make you feel better. Let's have it round the other way so's I can get a bit of light.

THE SEXTON *settles himself in the chair with his back to the audience. Whilst he is doing this,* KOORYATIN *paces the floor for inspiration, then seizes the pincers*

KOORYATIN: Now let's get started. Sit still, don't jerk, and it'll be over in the twinkling of an eye. What's important is that I get a good grip on it. [*He demonstrates with his hands*] That way the crown won't break. Now open your mouth.

He inserts the pincers and begins tugging. THE SEXTON*'s hands creep up* KOORYATIN*'s jacket, and he seizes his hands.* KOORYATIN *determinedly hangs on, and* THE SEXTON *curls one of his long legs round the back of* KOORYATIN*'s. He then slides his hands round* KOORYATIN*'s throat and begins squeezing. They struggle for a moment, locked in mortal combat. Then* KOORYATIN *staggers back, and* THE SEXTON *yells]*

VONMEEGLAZOV: I can't, I can't … Sainted fathers in heaven … Holy mother of God … Gracious Saint Peter … Lord have mercy. I can't, I can't …

KOORYATIN *stands clutching his neck and gasping for breath*

VONMEEGLAZOV *gives a terrible groan*

VONMEEGLAZOV: Gentle Saint Nicholas, I can't, I can't . . .

MASHA *pokes her head round the door*

MASHA: What IS going on in 'ere? I thought as someone was being murdered. [*recognizing* THE SEXTON, *she crosses herself and drops a deep bow*] Blessings of the Sabbath to you, Sexton. What yew doing 'ere?

STEPAN: He's come here for treatment that's what he's doing here.

MASHA: TREATMENT!!! [*gasps*] You're NOT letting Stepan Stepanich Kooryatin treat you, are you? [*hints*] Doctor's back in two days, you know.

THE SEXTON [*wails*]: Two days!! Two days of this pain??

MASHA [*hints*]: They do say as Mikhail Martinovitch the barber in the next village is very good at yanking out teef. My Mischa swears by him.

STEPAN: Will you be off about yore business and let me get on with mine.

MASHA: The Samovar's on the boil, Sexton. I'll make you a nice HOT cup of tea.

THE SEXTON *winces*

KOORYATIN [*threateningly*]: Will you stop busybodying in . . . [*but* MASHA *has fled*] Nosey old sow! [*He puffs angrily on his cigar*] It's no easy business you know, surgery – pulling teeth. [*pause*] The quicker we get on with it the quicker it'll be done. Are you ready?

THE SEXTON *nods mournfully*

KOORYATIN: Well, open yore mouth. Maybe it'd be better if you shut your eyes, then you won't know what's happening. [*He inserts the pincers and begins pulling*]

VONMEEGLAZOV*'s hands creep up and cover* KOORYATIN*'s*

KOORYATIN: Don't grab hold of my hands. Let go will yew, let GO I say.

THE SEXTON *let's go of* KOORYATIN*'s hands, and begins pummelling his chest with both fists as though he were kneading bread*

KOORYATIN *releases his hold under the onslaught*

VONMEEGLAZOV [*yells out*]: I can't, I can't ... No, I ...

KOORYATIN: Why you bellowing like a cow in labour. I ain't hardly got started yet.

VONMEEGLAZOV [*stunned*]: Hardly got started? [*beginning to get angry*] How long's it gonna take then – five years!!! [*He clutches his jaw and groans*] Sacred fathers ... hosts in heaven ... Angels! I can't I can't. [*He gets up from the chair and walks distractedly around the room, then sinks onto the stool*] Holy St. Michael ... Blessed Mary Magdalen ... It's all going dark in front of me eyes ... I don't think you know nothing about pullin' teeth.

KOORYATIN [*angry*]: Why d' you keep grabbing hold of my hands. I try to get a good grip and you keep pullin' me off course with your [*mocks*] "I can't I can't," and your stupid prayers. Blessed Saint Michael Ha!! He can't pull teef! I'm the one as can help you, not him.

VONMEEGLAZOV [*bitterly*]: No thank you very much. Thank you very much, but NO!

KOORYATIN: Idiot!

VONMEEGLAZOV: You're the idiot.

KOORYATIN: I had none of this bother with Squire Alexander Ivanovich Eegeepetski. He sat down on that stool, [*gesticulates*] didn't bat an eyelid nor make a sound, but then of course HE'S a different class of person – one of the gentry. THEY know how to behave. THAT'S the sort of person I like to deal with, not a village simpleton like you.

VONMEEGLAZOV: Simpleton yourself.

KOORYATIN: Knew all the professors in St. Petersburg, he did. "You know best Sergei Koozmich," he said, and with one quick jerk it was out.

VONMEEGLAZOV: Then why don't you do it like that with me, instead of hanging on – hanging on all the time like I was a dog on a string, making a meal out of it? [*He gets to his feet and paces the room*]

KOORYATIN: That's because you keep grabbing hold of me hands, another second and it would have been out. [*long pause*] [*persuasively*] Another second's all I need. That's all I need.

VONMEEGLAZOV [*sighs wearily*]: Oh all right then, get on with it. [*He makes the sign of the cross in front of the bottle of carbolic and seats himself*]

KOORYATIN: Let's have another look at it first. [*He takes* VONMEE-GLAZOV *by the shoulders and positions him. Then studies him for a long moment. He moves to the right, then moves to the left. Then he clambers over* THE SEXTON's *knees and practices how he'll do it*] [*mutters*] No, mebbe it'll be better from the other side. [*He clambers back over the knees*] It's no easy business you know, surgery. There's a bit more to it than your job, yanking bells in a church tower. It's a serious matter. You got to put yourself in the right position. There! That's it! Now – open yore mouth! I jest want to feel if it's getting loose. [*He pokes in his forefinger and shrieks as* THE SEXTON's *teeth sink into it.* THE SEXTON *releases him and he hops around the room, shaking his finger and yelping with pain*] You mangy cur. You bit me.

MASHA *pokes her head round the door*

MASHA [*innocently*]: Did someone call?

KOORYATIN: You been listening outside that door again, 'aven't you. Get back to your kitchen else I'll be reporting you to the doctor for interfering between me and the patients.

MASHA *quickly exits*

VONMEEGLAZOV [*groans*]: Blessed Virgin, I can't, I can't ...

KOORYATIN: That's it, then! I'm washin' my hands of the case.

VONMEEGLAZOV: I didn't mean it. It was you touching the nerve what made me bite you. Be your benevolent self, Sergei Koozmich. Take it out and let's be done with it.

Pause

KOORYATIN [*aggrieved*]: Oh, all right then. [*he crosses to* VONMEE-GLAZOV]

A long seesaw struggle begins, during which time VONMEEGLAZOV's *hands and legs creep up alternately, interspersed with* KOORYATIN *panting*

KOORYATIN: Sit still ... don't grab me hands ... it's comin' ... let go me hands ... that's it ... hold on now ... it's coming ... one more second ...

The tooth comes out and Kooryatin staggers back

KOORYATIN: Got it! [*panting*] You see ... there's more to it than leading the singing in church. But it's easy once you know how. Firm hands and skill are what you need. [*Sighs grandiosely*] Ay yes! As my friend the landowner said to me, "You've got skill, Sergei Koozmich" Called me by me first name he did – shook my hand.

VONMEEGLAZOV *sits stunned, gazing vacantly into space, his hands hanging limply between his knees*

KOORYATIN *crawls around the floor, muttering to himself*

KOORYATIN: Where did it go? ... Now, where did it go?

VONMEEGLAZOV's *eyelids begin fluttering. He shudders and groans, then runs his tongue round his mouth*

VONMEEGLAZOV: It's broken! ... You've broke it you hamfisted clod ... Half of it's still there.

KOORYATIN: What you talkin' about. What would a village gravedigger like you know about such matters. [*triumphantly*] Here it is! [*He picks up the fragment*] Oh! ... Oh yes ... Well, maybe if I was to try with the forceps, it'd ...

VONMEEGLAZOV *interrupts, his pathetic expression changed into one of extreme malice*

VONMEEGLAZOV: You mangy cur! You motheaten Devil! You bloated toad! How could they plant a wicked brute like you here to torment God loving Christians like myself. You bloodsucker! You ...

KOORYATIN [*discomfited, interrupts*]: Well, that's nice, I'm sure. Now you're showing yourself in your true colours. Is this all the thanks I get after making an extraction?

VONMEEGLAZOV: Extraction! Is that what you call it. May the Devil hisself perform a hundred such extractions on you when yet get to Hell, as you surely will, you flyblown sack of sheepdung! You spawn of Satan ...

KOORYATIN: Well! That's a nice way for a man of the cloth to talk I must say ... I didn't have to put up with this from Squire Alexander Ivanich Eegeepetski. He lived in St. Petersburg for six years he did, and he didn't call me no names. [*gaining confidence*] A hundred roubles apiece he paid for his suits – a heddicated man.

VONMEEGLAZOV: You pig's udder! You ... [*He groans and sinks back into his chair*] Oh, it's all going black in front of my eyes ... OOOOO!!

KOORYATIN [*becoming angry*]: What you howling like an old peahen for – you ain't dead are you?

VONMEEGLAZOV *rises menacingly from his seat, and* KOORYATIN *backs away*

VONMEEGLAZOV: Maybe you aint satisfied. Maybe you'd like ...

KOORYATIN: I'll get you some drops to ease the pain. [*He slams the study door behind him*]

MASHA [*bursts in*]: Where's Sergei Koozmi ... Ooh Sexton! You're as white as goats curd.

VONMEEGLAZOV *groans and begins tying the kerchief on top of his head*

MASHA: Has he done it?

VONMEEGLAZOV [*groans pathetically*]: He's broke it, the scabby mongrel.

MASHA: Well I can't say as I'm surprised. You should've ... [*She breaks off as* KOORYATIN *hurries in with a bottle of vodka and a large filled glass*]

KOORYATIN: That should soothe it for the time being, then maybe ...

VONMEEGLAZOV *snatches the glass and gulps down the vodka*

KOORYATIN: Have another dose, then maybe ... we could try with the forceps ...

VONMEEGLAZOV: Forceps!!!

MASHA: Forceps!

VONMEEGLAZOV [*menacingly approaching*]: If you think you pail of goats turds, that I'd ...

KOORYATIN *thrusts a glass of vodka into his hand*

VONMEEGLAZOV *tosses it back and sinks onto the stool, staring blankly ahead*

KOORYATIN [*mutters to* MASHA]: What yew doin' in here?

MASHA: There's a lad come from the Kooryatin Estate. Says as how the cow's started calving, and they need some help, urgent.

KOORYATIN [*relieved*]: Oh well ... well, I'd best be off then.

Vonmeeglazov bellows out a groan

KOORYATIN [*aside to* MASHA]: Have yew got any horseradish in the kitchen?

MASHA: Horseradish? Whatever for? I've never heard of them using that on a cow in labour.

KOORYATIN: It's for him you silly mare. They say if you soak horseradish in vodka, it's the best thing for an abscess. [*He pours out another stiff vodka*] Well I ... I ... [*He stuffs the bottle of vodka in his pocket and exits*]

THE SEXTON *totters back to the stool*

MASHA: That's right, you rest there a bit awhile, and then we'll try the vodka with the horseradish shall we? And if that don't work I'll get the gipsy pedlar to give you a lift to the next village. My Mischa swears by Mikail Martinovitch the barber for yanking out teeth ... [*polishing the instruments, grimaces at the blood stained knife*] And of course you COULD

81

try ewe's milk with cloves. And I heard tell only the other day of a soldier jut returned from the East who says down there they do use bulls urine to ease the pain. ... And of course there's always frog spawn rubbed into the gum at sunset ... But you have to do it on the last ray of the dying sun – else it don't work ... [THE SEXTON *ties his scarf round his head and staggers to the door.* MASHA *hasn't noticed* THE SEXTON*'s departure, and continues with her remedies*] And of course we could always try tying a piece of string on the stump, tying it to a doorknob and then slamming the door. ... That outside door's made of solid oak. [*She turns round to find* THE SEXTON*'s gone, calling after him*] Let's try tying a piece of string to the stump and then slamming the door.

She exits

MASHA [*voice off-stage*]: Sexton ... SEXTON ... Where's 'e got to?

Final curtain to rousing Russian folk song

"SWANSONG"

by

Anton Chekhov

(Translated and freely adapted by Elizabeth Gamberoni)

Characters in order of appearance

VASSILY-VASSILICH SVETLOVIDOV. (An elderly actor)

NIKITA. (A middle-aged prompt-master)

IGORKA, voice off

PETROUSHKA, voice off

The action takes place on the empty stage of a third rate provincial theatre, after the performance is over.

Backstage to the right, is a row of badly-made unpainted doors leading to the dressing rooms. Centre backstage to the left are piled up heaps of litter and two theatrical skips. Centre stage is one upturned stool.

It is night, and the building is silent, and in complete darkness. Somewhere in the distance a church bell chimes three o'clock. Silence. Then a glimmer of light can be seen, and VASSILY-VASSILICH SVETLO-VIDOV *comes on stage dressed as a jester, clutching a candle in his hand. He unsteadily walks a few paces, then stops and grimly laughs.*

SVETLOVIDOV: What a farce! What a joke! What's it come to when I fall asleep in my dressing room. The performance finished hours ago, everyone's gone home, and I, [*drily*] *I* in my imperturbable manner give a snoring recital. [*quietly*] You old fool Vassily Vassilich. You sour-tempered old fossil, you fleabitten old hound. It's come to something when you only have to sit in a chair to nod off – thanks to being tight. It doesn't say much for you, clever old dick! [*He bellows out*] Igorka. Igorka you devil. Petroushka. [*silence*] Those scoundrels are away somewhere sound asleep. May the devil breathe down their throats. May a hundred devils and a black witch breathe down their stinking throats!! [*He bellows louder*] "IGORKAAAAA ... [*He sighs, places the stool upright and seats himself on it, then places the candle carefully on the floor*] Nothing to be heard ... only the echo of my voice. Where have they got to? Three roubles apiece I gave those two villains today for looking after me so well. Huh! Not even a pack of hounds could scent them out now. They've well and truly gone and no doubt locked up the theatre behind them, the bastards. [*He shakes his head and flinches, then gingerly removes his jester's cap, and clasps his head tenderly*] "Oh my God! Drunk! Thanks to my benefit performance. Uggh! Lord alone knows how much wine and beer I must have poured down my gullet tonight. I ache all over. [*He pulls a sour face*] And it feels as if not one, but twenty furry tongues are roosting in my mouth. Uggh! Disgusting! [*long pause*] No more of these fourth rate farewell tours. Enough! Enough Vassily ... [*quietly*] enough! [*He grins wryly*] Stupid! To have guzzled down so much good stuff, you old nincompoop, and not remember the pleasure of drinking it. What a waste! [*groans*] Oh God be merciful – my back's breaking, my noddle feels as if it's been split down the middle, I can't stop shaking, and inside ... inside my heart feels as cold and dark as a tomb. If you have no consideration for your health, Vassily, you might at least have shown some pity for your age. [*pause*] Old age! ... Yes, Vassily Lad, face up to it – old age. However much you shuffle the cards, however brave a face you put on it, however much you prance around like a fool, you've had your life ... almost sixty eight years of it my venerable friend, and there's no getting it back now. You've drunk the bottle, and all that remains are the last few drops ... the sediment. So there it is – that is the way of it, and like it or not, Vassily old chap, it's time to start rehearsing the role of corpse. The Angel of Death awaits you in the wings ... [*He sits for a moment ruminating, then his attention is drawn to the empty auditorium*] Extraordinary! Even though I've been treading the boards for forty five years now, I do believe this is the first time I've ever seen a theatre at night like this, the very first time ... in complete darkness. Those dust sheets there like shrouds ... Curious that! [*laughs wonderingly*] Devil take it – that's strange! [*He picks up the candle, crosses to the ramp, and stares out at the darkened theatre*] Can hardly see anything ... Well, I can just about make out the Prompter's box, the conductor's rostrum, andddd ... [*he squints his eyes*] Ha ha! The Royal Box, in THIS fleapit! ... The rest is ... darkness. A black bottomless pit like a grave, in which lurks hidden, death itself, [*He shudders violently*] God it's cold! There's a draught blowing through this place like the wind down a chimney hearth. This is truly a place to summon up the dead. God damn it, it's uncanny. Ants are crawling up and down my spine. [*He shouts out*] Igorka ... Petroushkaaa ... Where have the devils got to? Devil take it. [*starts*] Why do I keep making mention of the evil one? [*He crosses himself*] Oh God, I will give up such language, give up the drink, I'm too old now, it's time to die. At sixty eight years others attend matins each morning, preparing to meet their maker, while I ... I ... Dear God, what must I look like with my ugly drunken mug, standing here mouthing obscenities in this ludicrous garb ... Get yourself changed, Vassily, get yourself changed. It's creepy in this place, you could die of fright if you were to spend the night here.

He begins hurrying towards his dressing room, just as a figure dressed in a long white dressing gown comes out of the furthest dressing room.
SVETLOVIDOV *lets out a shriek and stumbles back a few paces*

SVETLOVIDOV: Who are you? W-w-what have you come for? Whom have you come for. [*stamps his foot*] Who are you, God damn it!

NIKITA: It's erm ... it's me, Sir.

SVETLOVIDOV: Who's me?

NIKITA IVANICH [*approaches slowly, diffidently*]: It's me if you please, Vassily-Vassilich. It's me, Sir. I'm Nikita-Ivanich – the prompt master, Sir.

SVETLOVIDOV [*uncertainly lowers himself onto the stool. He is breathing heavily, and shaking all over*]: Oh my God! Who did you say you were? IS it really you Nikitoushka? What in God's name are you doing here at three o'clock in the morning?

NIKITA: I ... er, pass the nights here Sir, – in one of the dressing rooms. Only – erm, I'd take it as a great personal kindness, Sir, if you DIDN'T mention it to Aleksei-Fomitch, or I'll have nowhere to sleep ... As God is my witness I won't.

SVETLOVIDOV [*still clutching his heart*]: So it is you Nicky lad ... My God! Oh my God [*He regains his breath and studies* NIKITA *with a half smile*] Aleksei-Fomich tells me that you know most of the classics by heart, that only rarely do you need to consult the script. Is that so?

NIKITA [*embarrassed*]: Er, yes, that is so, Vassily-Vassilich. I – er, like to pride myself on that, Sir.

SVETLOVIDOV [*Nods his head in vigorous approval, and then winces*]: Good good! [*His mind goes to other things*] D'you know how many curtain calls I took tonight? Sixteen. Sixteen! They presented me with three huge bouquets, and other "tokens of their esteem" – everyone was in raptures over my performance, yet not one single soul could be bothered to wake up a drunken old man to make sure he got safely home. I'm old, Nicky lad – sixty eight years old ... I'm ill – fading away ... [*He clutches* NIKITA *to him and begins to weep*] Don't go, Nikitoushka. I'm old, frail, soon I must die ... It's terrible, terrible ...

NIKITA [*Tenderly, but deferentially*]: Come along, Sir, come along Vassily-Vassilich – it's time to go home, Sir.

SVETLOVIDOV: I'm not going. I haven't a home. No no no ...

NIKITA [*worried*]: Oh good gracious me. Have you even forgotten where you lodge, Sir?

SVETLOVIDOV: I'm not going there. I don't want to. I'm all alone there, not a soul comes nigh nor by, Nicky lad, I've no family, nor friends, not even a child ... I'm as solitary as the wind in the fields ... When I die there'll be no one to say prayers for me, no one to mourn ... I'm frightened to be on my own ... there's no one to comfort me, no one to keep me warm, no one to put me to bed when I get drunk. Who do I belong to? No one. Nobody, Nikitoushka, nobody loves me.

NIKITA [*Through tears*]: The public loves you, Sir. They love you Vassily-Vassilich.

SVETLOVIDOV: The public have gone home to sleep – they've forgotten about their "clown"! No ... nobody needs me, nobody loves me ... I've no wife, nor children ...

NIKITA [*interrupts*]: Come now. What a thing to grieve about!

SVETLOVIDOV [*fiercely*]: I'm a man, aren't I? I'm alive aren't I? It's blood flowing through my veins – not water. I'm of a good family, Nikitoushka – of a noble line! ... Before I fell into this pit, [*He indicates the theatre with a sweeping gesture*] I served in the Army – an Artillery Officer ... What a fine young man I was then. Handsome! Honourable! Loyal! Courageous! My God, what became of all that! And then by Christ, what a great actor I became! Wasn't I a great actor, Nikitoushka? [*Hanging onto* NIKITA*'s hand, he pulls himself to his feet*] What has become of it all? Where did all those years go to? My God, when I looked back just now into that pit, I remembered it all – everything! That black hole has gorged on forty five years of my life and swallowed it down. But what a life it was, Nikitoushka. Looking back on it now I can see it in smallest detail, as clearly as I see your face. Ah the rapture of youth. The enthusiasm! The optimism! The self confidence! The love of women. WOMEN, Nicky Lad.

NIKITA [*anxiously*]: I think it's time for you to go home, Vassily-Vassilich. Home to bed, Sir.

SVETLOVIDOV: Let me tell you something old fellow. When I was a young actor. When my fire was just beginning to emerge, I remember a woman who fell in love with me for my talent ... Graceful she was, elegant, slender as a poplar, young, innocent, pure – but ARDENT! As full of fire as a summer dawn. The darkest night could not have withstood the light of her blue eyes, her exquisite smile. [*He becomes very hammy, very melodramatic*] The waves of the mighty ocean are shattered on the rocks, but the waves of her hair with its little curling tendrils at the neck [*gesticulates*] could have destroyed cliffs, icebergs, snowdrifts ... [*quietly*] and then one evening I recall, I was standing before her as I stand before you now. How beautiful she was that night, as never ever before ... and she gave me a look that I will remember even beyond the grave – velvety it was, caressing, profound, full of the lustre of youth. I was enraptured, Nikitoushka, delirious. I fell on my knees before her and begged for her hand ... and ... she ... [*He continues in a lifeless voice*] and she replied, "Leave the stage ... Leave – the – stage. Do you understand?" She could love an actor, but become his wife, never! I remember that night I was playing some wretched farcical part, and as I was acting I felt that my eyes had been opened. I understood then that there's no such thing as sacred art, it's all gibberish – a fraud! I was for them a plaything, a slave, something to amuse them when they've nothing better to do – a clown, a Mountebank! THEN I understood the public, and from that day on I've never believed in their applause, nor in their flowers, or their wild enthusiasm. Ah yes, Nicky lad, they applaud me all right, and pay a rouble for my photograph. But I'm alien to them, dirt, trash, little more than a prostitute. Out of conceit they seek me out, trying to scrape up an acquaintance, BUT to humiliate themselves to the degree that they'd allow me to take one of their sister's or daughter's in marriage? Huh! That's another matter. No ... [*He lowers himself onto the stool and sighs heavily*] No, I don't believe in the public ... I don't believe in them!

NIKITA: You look dreadful, Vassily-Vassilich. You quite frighten me. Let me take you home. Come on Sir – be of good heart. [*He picks up the jester's hat*]

SVETLOVIDOV [*not listening*]: I saw through it all then ... and dearly that sight cost me. After that business ... after my experience with that young girl ... I began frittering my life away, I went off the rails, never looking to the future ... always playing the fool, jeering at everything, corrupting my mind, and you know Nicky Lad I WAS a true artist. What a gift I had! I wasted it all – debased my talent with foppish gestures and affected speech ... lost sight of the vision I once had. Lost all human dignity. [*He points an accusing finger at the darkened stalls*] That black pit has feasted on me and golloped me up ... I never realized it till today, but when I woke up and looked back at those sixty eight years behind me. Only now have I glimpsed old age. My song has been sung. [*sobs*] My song has been sung.

NIKITA: Vassily-Vassilich – dear old fellow ... My pigeon, ... please don't upset yourself ... Oh Lord! [*calls out desperately*] Petrooooshka. Igorka ...

SVETLOVIDOV: And yet what a gift I had. What power! You cannot imagine diction such as mine, so much feeling and grace, so many chords that were played in this one breast. [*He beats his chest*] It was enough to smother one. Listen to this old fellow ... Just let me get my breath. I'll do something for you from *Boris Godunov*. The "false" Tsarevich, speech, the false Dimitri! [*He breathes deeply, adopts a stance and recites*] That *I* before a haughty Polish maid should cringe! Think what she will – I AM Tsarevich, for the spirit of Ivan the Terrible from his grave proclaimed me so. "YOU shall be Dimitri," he said. And that same spirit has stirred his subjects to revolt and condemn-ed Boris to be sacrificed for my sake. [*He finishes reciting, and pauses*] Well?? Was THAT to be despised? [*In a lively manner*] "Just a minute, just a minute ... Something from *Lear* – why not! The sky is

black, you remember. Sheets of rain, Thunder! Berum
Berum! Lightning streaking the heavens, ZZZZZ! and
here: [*takes a deep breath*]
"Blow, winds, and crack your cheeks! rage! blow!
You cataracts and hurricanoes, spout!
Till you have drench'd our steeples. drown'd the cocks
You sulphurous and thought-executing fires,
Vaunt-couriers to oak-cleaving thunderbolts,
Singe my white head! And thou, all-shaking thunder,
Smite flat the thick rotundity o' the world!
Crack nature's moulds, all germens spill at once,
That make ingrateful man!"

SVETLOVIDOV [*pauses for a second, then stamps his foot*]: Come on,
come on, come on, Nicky lad. [*snaps his fingers*] Feed me
the line, feed me the line. Play the role of Fool.

NIKITA [*embarrassed, but delighted at the chance to act, dons the jester's
hat. He recites his lines with a country yokel's accent*]: "O
nuncle, court holy water in a dry house is better than this
rain water out o'door. Good nuncle, in and ask thy daughter's blessing: here's a night that pities neither wise man
nor fool."

SVETLOVIDOV: "Rumble they bellyful! Spit fire! Spout rain!
Nor wind, rain, thunder, fire, are my daughters:
I tax not, you elements, with unkindness;
I never gave you kingdom, called you children,
You owe me no subscription:
Then let fall your horrible pleasure;
[*his voice fades*] Here I stand your slave ... "
[*He pauses as the similarity of the words to his own situation strike
him*]

NIKITA [*thinking he has dried, prompts him*]:
"A poor, infirm, weak, and despised old man."

SVETLOVIDOV [*angrily*]: I know I know I know!!
[*He mutters*]: "A poor, infirm, weak, and despised old man."
[*then rather melodramatically acts out the lines*]:
"A poor, infirm, weak, and despised old man:
But yet I call you servile ministers,
that have with two pernicious daughters join'd

your high-engendered battle 'gainst a head
So old and wise as this! O! O! 'tis foul!''

[*He finishes reciting and smiles*]: Well? What about that? What
power! What talent! What consummate artistry! Some of
the old fire still remains, Nicky lad. Let's have something
more, something from another former triumph ... Let's
have ... a stab at ... [*ponders*] Ah yes! [*He gives a ringing
laugh*] Hamlet!! ... Now what shall it be? Yes, I'll begin. [*He
gestures magnanimously towards* NIKITA] You can play Guil-
derstein, Nicky lad. Ready? ''Ah, the recorders! Let me see
one. [*to* NIKITA] Why do you go about as if you would drive
me into a toil?''

NIKITA: ''Oh, my lord, if my duty be too bold, my love is too
unmannerly.''

SVETLOVIDOV: ''I do not well understand that. Will you play upon
this pipe?''

NIKITA: ''My lord, I cannot.''

SVETLOVIDOV: ''I pray you.''

NIKITA: ''Believe me, I cannot.''

SVETLOVIDOV: ''I do beseech you.''

NIKITA: ''I know no touch of it, my lord.''

SVETLOVIDOV: ''Tis as easy as lying: govern these vantages with
your fingers and thumb, give it breath with your mouth and
it will discourse most eloquent music. Look you there are
the stops.''

NIKITA: ''I have not the skill.''

SVETLOVIDOV: ''Why, look you now, how unworthy a thing you
make of me! You would play upon me; you would seem to
know my stops; you would pluck out the heart of my
mystery. Do you think I am easier to be played on than a
pipe? Call me what instrument you will, though you can
fret me, yet you cannot play upon me.'' [SVETLOVIDOV *roars
with delighted laughter, and applauds himself*] Bravo! Bis!
Encore! There was nothing of old age in that. To the devil
with old age, it's just stuff and nonsense! My fountain yet
still bubbles, Nicky lad, with youth, freshness, life and fire.

[*He squares his shoulders, draws in his stomach, and pats it*]
Where there is genius, Nikitoushka, old age doesn't exist!

NIKITA *torn with pity, watches* SVETLOVIDOV *as he struts across the stage*

SVETLOVIDOV [*turns, he is arrested by the expression on* NIKITA*'s face*]:
What is it? Have I robbed you of your wits? Overwhelmed
you? Taken your breath away? Wait a while, let me too have
a breather. [*he breathes deeply*] Then we'll have something
more gentle ... Dear God! Listen to Gogol's magical
words. What tenderness, so much delicacy, such music!
Shhh ... quiet.
"Quiet Ukranian night,
In the transparent sky the stars are bright.
Gladly the drowsy air doth welcome sleep.
No tremor stirs the silver poplar's leaves.
And ...

He is interrupted by the sound of heavy doors banging, and distant voices

SVETLOVIDOV: What's that?

NIKITA: It must be Igorka and Petroushka. [*Almost disappointed*]
They've come back ... Oh what great talent you have,
Vassily-Vassilich. Genius!!

SVETLOVIDOV [*accepts the compliment by inclining his head. He turns
in the direction of the banging door and calls out*]: "Igorka!
Petroushka! Come hither my falcons! [*grabs* NIKITA*'s arms*]
Come, let us get ourselves changed. [*They begin to cross the
stage,* SVETLOVIDOV *animatedly talking*] There's no such
thing as old age. It's all balderdash. Twaddle! [*He laughs
gaily, then pauses*] But why are you weeping, you dear kind
idiotic old ninny? Why are you blubbering? ... Come along
now, this won't do, this won't do at all. No no, old chap,
what a face to put on ... Why are you looking like that? [*In
tears, now himself,* SVETLOVIDOV *embraces* NIKITA] ... You
mustn't cry ... Where there's genius, where there's Art, old
age doesn't exist. No – nor loneliness, or pain – even death
itself is diminished. [*He weeps*] Yes, Nikitoushka, you're
right ... Our song has already been sung. Ha, what genius
am I talking about! I'm a sucked out lemon, a rusty nail, a

has-been. And you, dear promptmaster, you are a poor old theatrical drudge ... Come on – let's go. Let's have a drink! [*They continue towards the dressing rooms*] Huh! What talent!!! In a good production now, I'd be cast only as one of Fotinbras's retinue. [*laughs wryly*] And I'm even too long in the tooth for that. But there's no denying I'll miss it. [*He turns and looks back at the empty auditorium*] "Yes ... I shall miss it. D'you remember that scene in *Othello*, Nikitoushka? How does it go now?

"Farewell the tranquil mind! Farewell content!
Farewell the plumed troop, and the big wars,
That make ambition virtue! Oh farewell!
Farewell the neighing steed and the shrill trump,
the spirit-stirring drum, the ear-piercing fife,
The Royal Banner, and all quality, Pride, pomp,
and circumstance of glorious war! And, O you mortal engines,
whose rude throats Th'immortal Jove's dread clamours coun-
    terfeit,
Farewell!! Othello's occupation's gone."

NIKITA: Oh – such talent! Genius!!

SVETLOVIDOV: Or how about this? Most suitable!
"Away! And never to return! I flee from Moscow through the world to seek, where wounded heart may find a place to rest! A coach! Bring me my carriage."

A burst of drunken laughter from offstage, and a mocking voice mimics:

"Bring me my carriage" [*further laughter*] He makes you laugh, don't he!

A DIFFERENT VOICE [*jeers*]: What about my kingdom for a horse? [*further ribald laughter*]

SVETLOVIDOV [*hurt*]: Ah, what do those two fly-by-nights really know of the theatre ... Come my friend, let's just you and me have a drink together.

NIKITA: Oh Vassily-Vassilich, that would be most agreeable.

SVETLOVIDOV *puts his arm around* NIKITA*'s shoulder and they exit*

As the glimmer of the candle dies away, there is a slow final curtain

Recent JUVENTUS paperback publications available through all booksellers:

FROM *THE ITALIAN GIRL*
TO *CABARET*
(Aspects of Musical Humour,
Parody and Burlesque, by
G. Colerick).
182 Pages
ISBN 0 9524964 3 7
Published 1998

A timely addition to the rare list of modern books specialising in Musical Humour, with emphasis on the theatre. It researches and analyses unusual source material as well as familiar classics of comic opera and musical farces.

Elements of burlesque and parody may be found widely in today's entertainment, notably on T.V., but not often with imaginative use of fine music. The author has written about important exceptions, such as the cult movie, *Cabaret*, an Oscar Wilde send-up by Ken Russell, and a sophisticated Sondheim parody-musical.

"Without becoming too technical, the author shows how composers of intrinsically funny music achieve their effects ... An informative, diverting book for layman and musician alike." (Vilem Tausky, C.B.E.)

ROMATICISM & MELODY
(Essays for Music-Lovers by
George Colerick)
246 Pages
ISBN 0 9524964 2 9

A celebration of a superlative era of melody-making, from the 1820s to the 1950s, from Beethoven to Bernstein. The topics range from the early Brahms of the Piano Quartets to the use of Romantic music in Ken Russell's films, the young Bernard Shaw as music critic and Wagnerite, aspects of 20th century British music, Viennese and Parisian music theatre, Transylvanian folk-culture and of Soviet music policy within the Russian tradition. Over one half of the 26 chapters relate to the 20th century.

This book is 'in cumulative effect refreshing in its directness and enthusiasm ... full of comic and curious lore'. (BBC Music Magazine, November 1995)

In the first two years, it has taken its place in hundreds of libraries – public, music and school.